PSYCHOLOGY RESEARCH PROGRESS SERIES

A MULTIPLE SELF THEORY OF PERSONALITY

PSYCHOLOGY RESEARCH PROGRESS SERIES

Suicide and the Creative Arts
Steven Stack and David Lester (Editors)
2009. ISBN: 978-1-60741-958-7

Suicide and the Creative Arts
Steven Stack and David Lester (Editors)
2009. ISBN: 978-1-60876-560-7 (Online Book)

Jung Today: Volume 1- Adulthood
Francesco Bisagni Nadia Fina and Caterina Vezzoli (Editors)
2009. ISBN: 978-1-60741-893-1

Psychological Scientific Perspectives on Out of Body and Near Death Experiences
Craig D. Murray (Editor)
2009. ISBN: 978-1-60741-705-7

Jung Today: Volume 2- Childhood and Adolescence
Francesco Bisagni, Nadia Fina and Caterina Vezzoli (Editors)
2009. ISBN: 978-1-60741-894-8

Psychology Research Yearbook, Volume 1
Alexandra M. Columbus (Editor)
2009. ISBN: 978-1-60741-573-2

Psychology of Burnout: Predictors and Coping Mechanisms
Rachel V. Schwartzhoffer (Editor)
2009. ISBN: 978-1-60876-010-7

Perchance to Dream: The Frontiers of Dream Psychology
Stanley Krippner and Debbie Joffe Ellis (Editors)
2009. ISBN: 978-1-60876-123-4

Stress in the Year 2010 and Beyond
Michael F. Shaughnessy (Editor)
2009. ISBN: 978-1-60876-444-0

Neuropsychology of the Sense of Agency
Michela Balconi
2010. ISBN: 978-1-60876-358-0

A Multiple Self Theory of Personality
David Lester
2010. ISBN: 978-1-60876-783-0

PSYCHOLOGY RESEARCH PROGRESS SERIES

A MULTIPLE SELF THEORY OF PERSONALITY

DAVID LESTER

Nova Science Publishers, Inc.
New York

Copyright © 2010 by Nova Science Publishers, Inc.

All rights reserved. No part of this book may be reproduced, stored in a retrieval system or transmitted in any form or by any means: electronic, electrostatic, magnetic, tape, mechanical photocopying, recording or otherwise without the written permission of the Publisher.

For permission to use material from this book please contact us:
Telephone 631-231-7269; Fax 631-231-8175
Web Site: http://www.novapublishers.com

NOTICE TO THE READER

The Publisher has taken reasonable care in the preparation of this book, but makes no expressed or implied warranty of any kind and assumes no responsibility for any errors or omissions. No liability is assumed for incidental or consequential damages in connection with or arising out of information contained in this book. The Publisher shall not be liable for any special, consequential, or exemplary damages resulting, in whole or in part, from the readers' use of, or reliance upon, this material.

Independent verification should be sought for any data, advice or recommendations contained in this book. In addition, no responsibility is assumed by the publisher for any injury and/or damage to persons or property arising from any methods, products, instructions, ideas or otherwise contained in this publication.

This publication is designed to provide accurate and authoritative information with regard to the subject matter covered herein. It is sold with the clear understanding that the Publisher is not engaged in rendering legal or any other professional services. If legal or any other expert assistance is required, the services of a competent person should be sought. FROM A DECLARATION OF PARTICIPANTS JOINTLY ADOPTED BY A COMMITTEE OF THE AMERICAN BAR ASSOCIATION AND A COMMITTEE OF PUBLISHERS.

Library of Congress Cataloging-in-Publication Data
Lester, David, 1942-
  A multiple self theory of personality / David Lester.
    p. cm.
  Includes index.
  ISBN 978-1-60876-783-0 (hbk.)
  1. Personality. 2. Self. I. Title.
  BF698.L3968 2009
  155.2--dc22
                          2009044356

Published by Nova Science Publishers, Inc. ✦ New York

Contents

Preface		ix
Summary of the Postulates and Corollaries		xiii
Chapter 1	The First Postulate: The Mind as a Set of Subselves	1
Chapter 2	Executive Power	25
Chapter 3	The Varieties of Subselves	35
Chapter 4	Subselves and Group Dynamics	55
Chapter 5	Subselves and Psychological Disturbance	65
Chapter 6	Subselves and Psychotherapy	83
Chapter 7	Multiple Self Theory, Dissociation and Reincarnation/Possession	105
Chapter 8	The Construction and Description of the Multiple Self	121
Chapter 9	Developmental Considerations	135
Chapter 10	Applications of Subself Theory	145
Postscript		157
References		161
Index		173

PREFACE

This book presents a new theory of personality, and here I will explain how this theory came about.

The first point is that I have always been undecided whether to name it a "theory of personality" or "a theory of the mind." The problem is that, despite the fact that courses on "personality" are taught in almost every college and university by the psychology departments, and despite the fact that we psychologists know full well what theories fit into the textbooks we use, if I call it a "theory of personality," then critics will insist that I define the term "personality." The use of the term "personality" by psychologists is odd since it does not coincide with the dictionary definition of personality. "The state or quality of being a person" (Morris, 1976). What is that? Nor does it coincide with the lay use of the term: "A person of prominence or notoriety" (Morris, 1976).

My theory is, therefore, more properly called a "theory of the mind," in which case even my critics will not ask me to define the term "mind." However, the theory, if it is received with interest and judged to be important, may end up described in textbooks on theories of personality!

My background was in the natural sciences. Part 1 of my undergraduate degree at Cambridge University was in mathematics and physics. After a crisis of confidence, I joined the other "drop-outs" in the psychology department, and Part 2 of my degree was in psychology. Psychology at Cambridge University was "experimental psychology," meaning that we studied learning, perception, and physiological psychology. I emigrated to America and enrolled at Brandeis University for graduate study. Abraham Maslow who had founded the psychology department there was still in residence. Despite the fact that I had never heard of him prior to emigrating, and despite the fact that I was a self-assured "angry young man," I decided that he could be my mentor. He refused to teach graduate students then, at the end of his career, so I enrolled in one of his undergraduate courses (on utopias co-taught with Frank Manuel) and became his teaching assistant. He was also on my dissertation committee. Maslow introduced all of his students to the work of Andras Angyal and, as you will see, I came to believe that Angyal was one of the most important theorists of personality.

One of the first things I do on receiving any book on theories of personality is to check whether Angyal is mentioned. He rarely is. Yet, when I talk to well-established psychologists (meaning elderly), they typically agree that Angyal's theory of personality was one of the best. Angyal has two books, one written by himself while he was alive and the other edited by his colleagues after his death. Both are excellent, although that edited by his colleagues is the more readable.

But let me return to my background as a physicist. When I eventually came to study theories of personality, I was horrified. The textbooks typically had anywhere from ten to twenty chapters, one on each theory. How could there by twenty theories? In physics, I was used to two and at the most three theories of a phenomena. But twenty! That was bizarre. Nevertheless I studied them and, in my first few years as a professor, I taught them. After several years, however, I decided that I had to make sense of these competing theories. My graduate student notes were useless – they were made by that "angry young man." I re-read the theories and was relieved to discover that there were only three major theories of personality and, surprisingly (or perhaps not surprisingly), I had studied with one of them or with scholars who had just one degree of separation. The three theories were those of Sigmund Freud (I studied with Walter Toman, an Austrian psychoanalyst), George Kelly (I studied with the man himself), and Andras Angyal. These were the three most comprehensive theories, and I was unable to find any idea in any other theory (with one small exception) that could not be found in the theories of Freud, Kelly and Angyal. The result was a new set of lecture notes with which I felt comfortable and which resulted in my own book (Lester, 1995) – *Theories of Personality: A Systems Approach."*

The influence of Angyal and Kelly in the present theory is obvious. Not only does the holistic approach of Angyal dominate my subself theory of the mind, but I have imitated Kelly in laying out the theory as a series of postulates and corollaries. This requires another comment here. I published a preliminary and very short version of this subself theory of the mind in 2007 (Lester, 2007). When I began to write this book, I found that my system of postulates and corollaries in that article required drastic modification. The result is that the postulates and corollaries in this book differ greatly from those in my earlier article.

When I read other Prefaces, I note that authors often tell the reader what to expect in the subsequent pages and may even compare and contrast their theory or approach with those of others. I will not do that here. I will instead, thrust the reader into the first chapter knowing only that I am going to propose a theory of the mind that conceives of the mind as consisting of a set of subselves. I will compare and contrast my theory of the mind with other theories at the end of this book in a Postcript.

There is one final task for this Preface. What do I mean by the terms "personality" and "subself"? I am interested in intrapsychic theories – what is going on in our minds that explains our behavior. This I would define personality as follows:

> Definition: Personality consists of the hypothetical structures and processes in the mind that explain (1) the consistency of our behavior over time, (2) the inconsistencies in our behavior in different situations and from time to time, (3) the similarities between our behavior and that of others, and (4) the differences in our behavior from that of others.

Everyone with whom I have shared my ideas and who have given me feedback has insisted that I define "subself." In early drafts of this book, I did not do so, and I am reluctant to do so here. To define the term pins me down to only one definition, and I like the idea of leaving the term open to various definitions. We will see that other theorists have used terms such as subsystem, complex, syndrome, ego-state and subpersonality, just to name a few. I have compared subselves to roles in these pages (roles may be seen as the behavioral manifestations of subselves), and I also like to use computer programs such as Word, Excel and SPSS as analogies on occasion. However, other theorists have defined what they mean for their terms, and it easy to adapt these definitions to one for "subself."

> Definition: A subself is a relatively autonomous and organized set of psychological processes in the mind (such as thoughts, emotions and desires) that co-exists with other similar sets.

This is close to Maslow's definition of a syndrome (which was, however, a poor choice for a label): structured, organized complexes of diverse specificities (behavior, thoughts, impulses, perceptions and so on) that have a common unity (Lester, 1995, p. 122). I have omitted "behaviors" since behaviors are not in the mind but, of course, they are the result of the subselves. The organization of the subselves makes them "systems," and systems have system principles that characterize them. Thus, this multiple self theory of personality is a holistic theory.

SUMMARY OF THE POSTULATES AND COROLLARIES

DEFINITION: Personality consists of the hypothetical structures and processes in the mind that explain (1) the consistency of our behavior over time, (2) the inconsistencies in our behavior in different situations and from time to time, (3) the similarities between our behavior and that of others, and (4) the differences in our behavior from that of others.

DEFINITION: A subself is a relatively autonomous and organized set of psychological processes in the mind (such as thoughts, emotions and desires) that co-exists with other similar sets.

POSTULATE 1: The mind can be conceptualized as consisting of several subselves

COROLLARY 1a: Not every individual has a multiple self.

COROLLARY 1b: Having a unified self or a multiple self has no bearing on the individual's psychological health.

POSTULATE 2: At any point in time, one subself is in control of the mind. It may be said to have executive power.

COROLLARY 2a: When one subself has executive power, the other subselves are said to be suspended

COROLLARY 2b: When one subself has executive power, some of the other subselves may be monitoring what is being processed by the executive subself, but others may not. Clinical investigation of the individual is necessary to determine which subselves are monitoring the executive subself and which are not.

COROLLARY 2c: A subself may have executive power for anywhere from seconds to hours or longer.

COROLLARY 2d: Selfhood is whichever subself has executive power at the time.

COROLLARY 2e: The existence of subselves accounts for the occasional inconsistency in the behavior of individuals. The behavior of an individual may differ when each subself has executive power.

COROLLARY 2f: Subselves can account for the co-existence of two conflicting desires or forces in the mind.

POSTULATE 3: There are several possibilities for subselves that are common to all individuals.

COROLLARY 3a: One common set of subselves consists of one or more core selves and one or more façade selves.

COROLLARY 3b: For some people, the façade self may become so pervasive that people come to believe that it is their real self

COROLLARY 3c: Other common sets of subselves are the topdog/underdog, introjected subselves and regressive subselves.

COROLLARY 3d: Subselves may be defined in terms of social group membership or personality attributes and, in some people, there may be mixed types.

COROLLARY 3e: Some subselves may occur in pairs with complementary attributes, whereas other subselves may occur in pairs with similar attributes. It is a clinical question as to whether individuals have such pairs, what is the genesis of these pairs and why some complement each other while others do not.

POSTULATE 4: The subselves function in a manner similar to a small group of individuals.

COROLLARY 4a: Some subselves collaborate in groups or teams, while others may be isolates; some appear in many situations while others may appear on only rare, special occasions; some are domineering while others are submissive.

COROLLARY 4b: Subselves may form coalitions within the larger group. These coalitions may improve or impair the functioning of the mind.

COROLLARY 4c: In some productive organizations of subselves, one subself acts as a leader, analogous to the conductor of an orchestra, coordinating the contributions of the other subselves.

COROLLARY 4d: Egalitarian groups of subselves typically result in greater satisfaction for the individual.

COROLLARY 4e: The individual's subselves can reorganize themselves in new ways as they develop and as the situation changes.

COROLLARY 4f: Groups of subselves are best limited to at least four and to no more than ten.

COROLLARY 4g: Multiple selves may lead to more rational decisions than a unified self in some situations.

COROLLARY 4h: The interactions between multiple selves may be usefully described using the concepts that have been proposed to describe family dynamics.

COROLLARY 4i: Groupthink can be avoided by assigning at least one subself to the role of devil's advocate.

POSTULATE 5: There are many forms of psychological disturbance which can arise from the conceptualization of the mind as consisting of many subselves.

COROLLARY 5a: The system principle of a subself may be pathological.

COROLLARY 5b: Psychological disturbance can arise from symptoms of pressure, intrusion, and invasion between subselves.

COROLLARY 5c: Psychological disturbance can arise when one subself has executive power exclusively.

COROLLARY 5d: It can be healthy for one subself to maintain overall control of the group of subselves while allowing each subself to have executive power from time to time or delegating duties to other subselves. It may be pathological when this "chairman of the board" is impaired in its role, for this may lead to conflict, struggles and even war between the subselves, rendering the person's mind chaotic.

COROLLARY 5e: Psychological disturbance can arise when the individual has difficulty setting and shifting set (changing which subself has executive power) appropriately in a situation.

COROLLARY 5f: Psychological disturbance can arise when the content of the subselves is pathological.

COROLLARY 5g: The healthiest individuals may have one subself that is in charge of the set of subselves.

COROLLARY 5h: Some subselves may cease to be useful as the individual matures and may need to become less influential in determining the individual's life.

COROLLARY 5i: Subselves that may be unhelpful for some tasks and impair performance and development may be useful in other situations.

COROLLARY 5j: The possibility of attributing negatively-valued aspects (thoughts, desires, emotions or behaviors) of oneself to one or more subselves may enable the individual to maintain high self-esteem since the negative aspects of one subself do not color the other subselves.

POSTULATE 6: The concept of subselves is useful for psychotherapy and counseling.
  COROLLARY 6a: One useful tactic in psychotherapy is to have the client identify and provide names for their subselves.
  COROLLARY 6b: Some subselves are more useful in the psychotherapeutic process than others
  COROLLARY 6c: It is important in psychotherapy to know the relationships among a client's network of subselves, that is, the alliances and coalitions that exist and how they change from time to time and situation to situations.
  COROLLARY 6d: Some subselves may become enmeshed, and the psychotherapist must help the client create sufficiently impermeable boundaries. Alternatively, some subselves may become disengaged, and the task then is to recognize them and encourage them to express themselves.
POSTULATE 7: Some subselves may be in a dissociated state about which the other selves have delusional, minimal or no knowledge.
  COROLLARY 7a: The concept of dissociated subselves can explain such phenomena as multiple personality, possession, mediumship, reincarnation and auditory hallucinations.
POSTULATE 8: Kelly's REP Grid technique may be useful for describing and measuring the content of subselves.
POSTULATE 9: The set of subselves that constitute the mind of an individual changes with age
  COROLLARY 9a: There are subselves formed by the introjection of the desires and thoughts of powerful others (in particular, parental figures) and imitation of their personality and behavioral styles
  COROLLARY 9b: Subselves may be formed as a result of early experiences.
  COROLLARY 9c: Subselves may be formed by the encountering of possible subselves exemplified by other people.
  COROLLARY 9d: There are probably regressive subselves in most, if not all, individuals which are the subselves that they had at an earlier stage in life.
  COROLLARY 9e: Individuals can seek to create new subselves for the future
  COROLLARY 9f: Individuals form fewer possible selves as they age. Aging narrows the possibilities for the individual as he or she moves toward completing their specific system principle.
  COROLLARY 9g: Subselves are selected to become more or less permanent members of the multiple self depending on their usefulness in helping the individual succeed.
POSTULATE 10: The individual eventually tries to integrate the subselves.

COROLLARY 10a: The integration of subselves is a task for the second half of life.
COROLLARY 10b: One form of integration is the elimination of all subselves but one.
COROLLARY 10c: One form of integration is the fusion or merging of the separate subselves into a single unified self.
COROLLARY 10d: One form of integration is peaceful and harmonious co-existence, cooperation and collaboration between the subselves.
COROLLARY 10e: It is a clinical issue as to which individuals choose each path of integration and what determines this choice.

Chapter 1

THE FIRST POSTULATE:
THE MIND AS A SET OF SUBSELVES

> Accordingly it is not surprising that some people have great resistance to seeing their personality as other than one monolithic coherent unit. Something inside them resists the awareness that their personality is made up of many different parts - as if to admit such a breakdown would cause the breaking down into non-being of their identity itself. (Vargiu, 1974, p. 53)

Many of the major theorists of personality have proposed that the mind is made up of many subselves. For example, Eric Berne (1961) talked of ego states, Carl Jung (Progoff, 1973) of complexes, Abraham Maslow (1970) of syndromes, Gordon Allport (1961) of traits, Henry Murray (1959) of themata, and Andras Angyal (1965) of subsystems. However, despite this agreement on the usefulness of the concept of the subself, very little theoretical discussion has appeared using this concept. The present book explores the past use of the concept and proposes postulates and corollaries for a formal multiple self theory of the mind.

Other scholars interested in this topic have taken a cognitive approach to the multiple self (e.g., Higgins, Klein & Strauman, 1985) or focused on scales to measure aspects of self-complexity (e.g., Campbell, Trapnell, Heine, Katz, Lavallee & Lehman, 1996), and they seek to ground their writings in the earlier ideas of William James (1890) and George Mead (1934). The present book however, is grounded in the major of theories of personality which are usually ignored by these other approaches.

It should be noted that many writers appear to be talking of the *structure* or the *architecture* of the personality or the mind, but close examination indicates that they are not. For example, Cervone (2005) entitled his article "Personality

Architecture," but his examples include the five factor-model (McRae & Costa, 1999). The five-factor model simply proposes five basic dimensions (or traits) of personality. Individuals may have profiles on these five-factors, much as they can on the MMPI, but there is no organization or structure. In contrast, Eric Berne's ego states have structure and interactive properties. It is this type of "architecture" that the present theory explores.

Postulate 1: The Mind Can Be Conceptualized as Consisting of Several Subselves

The notion that the mind can be conceptualized as consisting of several subselves has been proposed by many theorists in the past. In this section, the ideas of a few of these theorists will be briefly reviewed.

SUBSELVES IN THE MAJOR THEORIES OF PERSONALITY

Carl Jung

Jung's term for the totality of psychological processes was the psyche. Jung proposed that complexes exist within the psyche, autonomous partial systems that are organizations of psychic contents. Complexes are subsystems of the whole. (The complexes in the collective unconscious are the archetypes.) In particular, Jung identified several complexes that he felt were of particular use for a discussion of human behavior.

The ego consists of our conscious psychic contents and contains percepts, memories, thoughts, desires, and feelings. The persona is a subsystem within the ego and is the self that we present to others, the mask we wear in daily intercourse with others. It consists of the roles we play in our lives.

The shadow consists of those psychic contents in the personal (and to some extent the collective) unconscious that are in opposition to the contents of the ego. These contents are less developed and less differentiated than the contents of the ego, but their presence is made apparent to the ego whenever the boundaries between the systems break down and the contents from the shadow intrude into the ego.

In addition, the subsystem in the collective unconscious that is in opposition to the persona subsystem of the ego is called the anima in males and the animus in females. By modern standards, Jung erred here in identifying the core of human behavior in terms of the sexual stereotypes of his day. Jung described males as "masculine" and females as "feminine," in what today would be considered a gender-biased fashion. For example, Jung described the unconscious animus of females as rational and discriminating, showing that Jung believed females to have an irrational and emotional conscious ego. Today, there is no need to accept all of Jung's ideas wholesale. The anima and animus can be conceptualized more appropriately as the subsystems of the shadow that are in opposition to the persona, and their content can vary depending upon the psychic contents of the particular persona. (Perhaps these should both be called "animum," using the Latin neuter gender?)

Eric Berne

Whereas psychoanalytic theory usually uses the terms id, ego, and superego to characterize particular wishes, Eric Berne (1961) followed Paul Federn (1952) and Edoardo Weiss (1950) in defining ego states. An ego state is a coherent system of feelings and behavior patterns. Complete ego states can be retained in the memory permanently. The defense mechanisms can operate upon complete ego states and, for example, ego states can be repressed as a whole. Ego states from earlier years remain preserved in a latent state, with the potential to be resurrected (recathected in Berne's terminology).

The Parent ego state is a judgmental ego state, but in an imitative way (primarily, of course, by imitating the person's parents). It seeks to enforce borrowed standards. The Parent ego state parallels the superego in psychoanalytic theory. The Adult ego state is concerned with transforming stimuli into information and then processing that information. It corresponds to the ego in psychoanalytic theory. The Child ego state reacts impulsively, using prelogical thinking and poorly differentiated and distorted perception. It corresponds to the id in psychoanalytic theory. However, although this simple correspondence is worth noting, the id, ego, and superego are sets of wishes (Toman, 1960), while the Child, Adult, and Parent are integrated and coherent ego states. People are always in some ego state, and they shift from one to another (a process which Angyal [1941] called setting and shifting set).

Abraham Maslow

Abraham Maslow (1970), one of the important influences in the development of the field of humanistic psychology, urged a holistic approach to the study of personality. Behavior, he argued, is as an expression or creation of the whole personality, which in turn is the result of everything that has ever happened to it. Personality is composed of syndromes, that is, structured, organized, and integrated complexes of diverse specificities (behavior, thoughts, impulses, perceptions, and so on) that have a common unity. The total personality and the syndromes tend to be well-organized and to resist change, instead seeking to re-establish themselves after forced changes and to change as a whole because of tendencies to seek internal consistency. Maslow's use of the term syndrome is a confusing term because in psychiatry it refers to a cluster of symptoms associated with a particular psychiatric disorder.

Within each syndrome there are hierarchies of importance and clusterings. There are specificities whose occurrences are associated, that is, thoughts and impulses that are frequently found together. Maslow felt that to analyze these elements lower in the hierarchy of organization was similar to studying an object at different levels of magnification. For example, we may study the tendency to prejudice, which is a subsyndrome of the need for power, which is a subsyndrome of a general insecurity syndrome. Although such analyses examine atomistic elements, Maslow preferred to study the elements in context rather than in isolation.

Behavior is an expression of the whole integrated personality (and thus, an expression of all of the personality syndromes). Your laughter at a joke, for example, is affected by your intelligence, self-esteem, energy, and so on. It is an expression of your whole personality.

Gordon Allport

Gordon Allport (1961) noted that the most important fact about personality was that it had a relatively enduring and unique organization, and the critical question concerned its structure and composition. This proposition clearly cast Allport as a holistic theorist. Indeed, he specifically rejected the view that a personality was merely a sum of certain elements.

Allport distinguished five levels in the structure of personality:

1. Conditioned reflexes -- simple learned forms of adaptive behavior
2. Habits -- integrated systems of conditioned responses
3. Traits -- dynamic and flexible dispositions resulting in part from the integration of specific habits
4. Selves -- systems of traits with coherence

5   Personality -- the progressive final integration of all the systems of response

Allport (1955) added another level to his hierarchy, called intentions, complex core characteristics of personality. Intentions are rather like a philosophy of life or a value system (perhaps analogous to what Andras Angyal called a system principle). These have a dynamic effect on our changing personality and set the goals toward which we strive. The unfinished structure of our personality has a dynamic power, tending toward closure as we age. Most of us can be characterized by a few major intentional characteristics, unique for each of us, which guide the smaller units of our personality so that they are consistent with these major intentions.

Allport used the term proprium for the core self. "The proprium includes all aspects of personality that make for inward unity" (Allport, 1955, p. 40); it is "the central interlocking operations of the personality" (Allport, 1955, p. 54). It appears to exclude inherited dispositions and characteristics acquired by learning such reflexes, habits, skills, and cultural values (unless these become integrated into the proprium).

Allport gave the proprium eight properties: (a) a bodily sense, i.e., streams of sensation from within the organism, (b) a self-identity, (c) ego-enhancement, a self-seeking tendency, (d) ego-extension through possessions, loved objects, ideal causes, and loyalties, (e) a rational agent, (f) a self-image, both what we are and what we aspire to, (g) propriate strivings that maintain rather than reduce tension, similar to Maslow's growth motives, and that make for the unification of the personality, and (h) a knower, a cognizant self that transcends these other functions.

Allport is most well-known for his focusing on traits, but many textbooks misrepresent his position on this concept. Allport is often called a trait theorist because he also became interested in measuring traits that are found to be common to all people. However, this was a side issue. Allport defined a trait as a "generalized and focalized neuropsychic system (peculiar to the individual)" with the capacity to "initiate and guide consistent...forms of adaptive and expressive behavior" (Allport, 1937, p. 295). Traits for Allport are unique for each person, and a trait is an organized subsystem in the personality. It is similar to the subsystem of Angyal and the complex of Jung. In his later writings, Allport changed the term to personal disposition.

All traits are directive tendencies, but not all directive tendencies are traits. Traits are generalized and enduring; they have less to do with fleeting mental sets than with lasting processes such as interests, tastes, complexes, sentiments, and ideals. Traits result from an integration of numerous specific habits and a fusion of these habits with endowment. A trait forces the formation of new habits, useful for the trait, thereby transcending its specific foci of origin. Traits become autonomous motivational systems basic to the personality. No two people ever have precisely the same trait.

Traits are always changing and depend closely on the fluid conditions of the environment. Indeed, to be successful, traits must be dynamic and capable of changing. Traits can also be directive (or motivational) or stylistic (or expressive). (Expressive traits generally have a greater unconscious component.) Traits can also overlap, that is, they are interdependent, and they can also be in conflict. A trait is identified, not by a clean-cut boundary, but rather by a nuclear focus.

A trait can become so pervasive and dominant in someone's life that it is called a cardinal trait. More often, several central traits direct the personality, supported by a number of secondary traits. Allport felt that people have a limited number of traits, perhaps 5 to 10. Clearly, this is analogous the ideal number of subselves for a healthy mind (see Chapter 4, Corollary 4f, later in this book).

Allport noted that an environment that places few demands on a person makes it easier to develop an integrated unified personality. The stresses of life may make it difficult (if not impossible) to adequately integrate a personality. Sometimes there is inertia in the person that impedes integration. Integration requires a strong desire in the person or an insistent demand from the environment for change.

Under strong environmental pressures, regression, in which the personality reverts to an earlier level of integration, may sometimes occur. Dissociation may take place when a self-coherent system in the personality fails to integrate with the remaining parts of the personality. Sometimes infantilism, or a failure to develop, occurs.

Allport saw the mind as a unified system, and he considered which factors help provide this unity. The baby has a primitive unity because it has not yet differentiated. However, once differentiation takes place, then integration must occur between the various parts. Homeostasis, especially physiological homeostasis, in which the system tends to persist in a steady state and to preserve it, leads to a static kind of unity. In convergence, one task comes to dominate the person and this provides a temporary unity, much as a cardinal trait facilitates a more long-term unity. Allport also noted that the very term self, a sense of which evolves in each of us as we develop, implies unity. The mature person can be self-objective and has a unifying philosophy of life (c.f., Angyal's version of the general system principle in Chapter 3).

Many presentations of Allport's ideas minimize the holistic aspects of his theory, focusing instead on his development of the concept of trait. From there, the writer typically moves on to the measurement of traits by modern psychological tests and the formal concepts of reliability and validity in modern measurement theory (e.g., McAdams, 1994). Although measurement issues interested Allport to some extent, we must not ignore the fact that Allport's concept of a trait was very similar to the notion of a subsystem or subself. For example, a cardinal trait can be seen as analogous to a core role for a person. Furthermore, integration of the structures of the mind into a unified whole was seen by Allport as a major goal for humans, and his term for this unified whole, the proprium, is identical to what Jung called the self.

Kurt Goldstein

Kurt Goldstein (1963a, 1963b) proposed a theory of personality based upon his experience with the behavior and rehabilitation of brain-damaged patients. He felt that pathological phenomena are modifications of a normal process and, hence, can indicate the lawfulness of the normal process. (It is a common assumption in psychology that we can come to an understanding of psychological processes by exploring how they break down or how they manifest themselves in alternative organisms, such as lower animals.)

Goldstein's major assumption is that the person functions as a whole. Despite the fact that often our work with clinical patients or with animals in a laboratory situation suggests that discrete, circumscribed, disparate disturbances can be observed, Goldstein felt that this conclusion was wrong and a result of observing the organism in an abnormal situation. Symptoms resulting from pathology or laboratory manipulation are not isolated phenomena. Rather, they are solutions tried by the modified organism to cope with the new specific demands. The symptoms are expressions of the total organism and involve widespread changes. In a similar vein, Goldstein considered mind and body to be merely different aspects of unitary life process.

The mind is differentiated into part members, but it does not consist of these members. The members do not struggle against each other, nor does the whole struggle against the members. The members we distinguish neither compose the mind, nor are they antagonistic to it. This can be seen as a primitive statement of the notion of subselves.

Kurt Lewin

Kurt Lewin (1935, 1936) stressed that the mind was a temporally extended whole and not a set of rigid connections of distinct pieces or elements. The mind is dynamic because forces in the mind and the environment are changed by the process of interaction. The whole is continuously changing under the influence of internal and external forces.

Because the mind is a unified whole, the proper questions of personality concern the structure of the whole, the interactions of subwholes, and the boundaries between subwholes. For example, subwholes may not have clear communication with one another. The communication may be weak or nonexistent. Without some segregation between subwholes, ordered action would be impossible. In addition, some subwholes may be considered "central" whereas others are "peripheral." The effect of subwholes on the person is primarily determined through the whole in which they are embedded.

Lewin proposed that psychological processes have a tendency toward equilibrium. The process changes, however, so that the system as a whole moves toward equilibrium, though part processes may go in opposite directions (c.f., Jung's concept of balance discussed in Chapter 3, Corollary 3e). Systems in equilibrium may also have residual tensions, as does a spring under tension. This requires subsystems with firm boundaries and actual segregation of the systems from their environment.

People differ in the number of subsystems in their mind, that is, the degree of differentiation. First, the child is less differentiated (or stratified) and has fewer subsystems than the adult. Second, the dynamic material of the subsystems may also be different. Subsystems can differ in fluidity and rigidity, for example, and systems can change with different amounts of ease (suddenly versus gradually; c.f., set and shifting set in Eric Berne's theory, discussed earlier). Children's subsystems are, on the whole, more fluid than those of adults. Third, the content of subsystems may differ. This may be crucially determined by life experiences. Finally, the subsystems may be relatively harmonious or in conflict. The self or ego was seen by Lewin as one subsystem of the whole. He saw this self as roughly equivalent to the conscious region of the mind.

Marked differences exist between people in the tempo, extent, and age limits of differentiation, as well as in the tempo and extent of the stiffening of psychological material. In the retarded, differentiation proceeds more slowly and ceases (or begins to decline) earlier. Individuals differ in which parts differentiate most (for example, intellectual versus non-intellectual parts) and in the functional significance of different parts (does a part play a primary or secondary role in one's life?).

Very fluid systems will differentiate very easily momentarily. However, the slightest force will alter the structure so that development of a relatively permanent differentiated structure is difficult. At the other extreme, functional rigidity with respect to changes hinders differentiation. Lewin thought that the rate of differentiation might be either an inherited predisposition or acquired as a result of life experiences.

In general, Lewin argued that a system is more strongly unified if it contains fewer parts or subsystems, if the subsystems are less separated from one another, if the structural arrangement of the subsystems promotes unification (for example, if each subsystem interacts with every other subsystem rather than in a linear chain), and if the whole system is more strongly separated from the environment. States of great inner tension also bring about unification of the mind.

A person's structure remains relatively constant over a long period of time. But sudden changes can occur as, for example, when a person falls in love or undergoes a religious conversion. Parts of the system can also separate themselves off and develop relatively independently. This sometimes occurs in healthy people, but more often in the mentally ill. Lewin suggested that newly developed subsystems have less firm boundaries than older subsystems. Thus, under external stimulation, a more unified reaction occurs. Changes in the fluidity of the system caused by factors such as fatigue have a similar effect.

Interestingly, Lewin has had more influence on social psychology than on theories of personality, probably because many of his students went on to work in that particular field.

Henry Murray

Henry Murray never proposed a theory of personality in the sense that other theorists have. Rather, he took the theories proposed by others and formed an amalgam of them, so that his writings are somewhat like an introduction to human behavior written in general terms.

Murray (1959) listed those disciplines and theorists that influenced his theory of personality. From Freud, Murray adopted the division of psychological material into conscious and unconscious parts and a belief in the importance of early experiences for the development of personality. He also found the organismic, holistic, or molar conceptions of personality useful, although not rejecting completely the usefulness of focusing at times on the elements that make up the whole. Murray's preference was to conceptualize the organization of the parts as hierarchical systems with vertical integrations of superordinate and subordinate parts. Murray's analyses of the elements focused mainly upon needs and subneeds (subordinate components of a larger system of need-aims), and dispositions (sentiments, interests, attitudes, and evaluations).

In an early statement of his theory, Murray (1938) stressed the wholeness of humans at birth, after which they begin to differentiate into parts. The whole and the parts are mutually related and cannot be understood separately. Furthermore, there is a temporal unity. The history of the person is the person. Eventually, conflict between the parts occurs and, with increasing age, conflict resolution, synthesis and creative integration back into a unified whole again. Murray proposed that psychic events or processes that govern our behavior at each moment in time, be called regnant processes or regnancies. Regnancies may be conscious or unconscious.

Sequences in which press (environmental forces) are followed by needs, thereby resulting in behavior (or in Murray's terminology actones), were called thema. A succession of such episodes is called a complex thema. If a person has characteristic modes of behavior, in which certain press (environmental forces) result in characteristic needs and characteristic behaviors, Murray referred to this as a need integrate or complex. Behaviors that result from internal needs are proactive, whereas those that result from external press are reactive.

OTHER PROPOSALS FOR SUBSELVES

Anderson and Carter

Koestler (1967) introduced the concept of a *holon*, an entity that is simultaneously a part and a whole. A holon is made of parts of which it is the whole, but it is also a part of some larger whole of which it is but one component. Koestler named the entity after the Roman god Janus who faced in two directions at the same time. Applying this concept to human behavior, Anderson and Carter (1974) noted that the behavior, for example, of a family, is not determined by one holon acting in isolation, but rather by the interaction and mutual causation of all of the holons.

Anderson and Carter noted that suppressing one subsystem may be preferable to permitting that subsystem to be unchecked. For example, in the psychoanalytic defense mechanisms, certain desires are suppressed and repressed, and this may be better than allowing them free expression for the satisfaction of these desires may imperil the person's existence.

"Organzation refers to grouping and arranging of parts to form a whole, to a putting into working order" (Anderson & Carter, 1974, p. 16). Carter and Anderson noted that the traditional view of psychoanalytic theory, which views the id, ego and superego as "psychic structures," requires that the three subsystems work in harmony with the ego dominant. Erikson's (1968) stage of identity versus diffusion, can be viewed, according to Anderson and Carter, as organization versus disorganization. During this identity crisis, identity requires drawing the components or facets of one's personality together to form an organized, working whole. In diffusion, there is disharmony or randomness among the component parts of the personality.

Wholes can achieve balance. Anderson and Carter argued that balance is not a static or fixed state, but a dynamic state, changing with time. The term equilibrium implies a fixed point of balance, like a see-saw, in which any disturbance eliminates the balance. Homeostasis implies a more variable balance, suggesting a range of limits within which balance can be restored, like a person riding a motor cycle who must adjust to the speed of the bike, the road surface, bends in the road, the wind and the movement of the passenger sitting behind.

Anderson and Carter noted that systems must shift their balance between changing their structure (morphogenesis to use a term coined by Buckley [1967]) and maintaining the *status quo* (morphostasis). If the entity maintains its identity, then we can say that it has achieved a steady-state – it has continuity with past states and will have continuity also with future states. Susbsystems have boundaries which permit interchange of communications between one another. Boundaries are, therefore, not barriers.

Subsystems may are also arranged vertically or hierarchically. Some subsystems give approval of decisions or impose sanctions, others control the communication of information, while still others may determine the sequence with which the subsystems contribute to a decision. Anderson and Carter noted that subordination-superordination and dominance-submission refer to this hierarchical organization. Some subsystems, however, may remain relatively autonomous from this hierarchical organization. In the dissociative state of multiple personality, for example, some subsystems resist integration into the organized whole and function autonomously.

Miller (1965) noted that in most organizations of subsystems, each subsystem has some autonomy and some subordination or constraint, both from lower level and from higher level components, thereby demonstrating their holon characteristics.

In differentiating, the functions are divided and assigned to the parts of the whole. Specialization adds the stipulation that a particular component performs only a specific function and that no other component performs that same function. As differentiation and specialization become more characteristic of a system, then linking between the subsystems and free and full communication become more important.

Decision Theorists: Self-Deception

Those concerned with rational decision-making, such as economists, psychologists, and philosophers, have been concerned with the ability of people to deceive themselves. Although Elster (1985) drew attention to inconsistencies in people's beliefs and wishes, he preferred the explanatory concept of mental compartmentalization rather than split selves. For others (for example, Pears, 1985), self-deception appears to involve two selves, the subject and the object of deception. Writers on this issue typically consider the problem to be one self ignoring the "truth" perceived by the other self. Pears warned against confusing these two selves with the conscious and the unconscious and instead proposed the concept of functional insulation. The subject-self contains elements that do not interact with all of the object-self's elements. The two systems can be conceptualized as overlapping circles. Pears viewed the subject-self as "a small temporary system, like a camp set up for the duration of a particular campaign and then abandoned, and the force that splits it off from it is an ordinary wish" (Pears, 1985, p. 77). The desire to avoid accepting what the requirement of total evidence counsels causes this functional isolation (Davidson, 1985).

Others, in discussing the phenomenon of self-deception, have proposed a model of the mind of "the older medieval city, with relatively autonomous neighborhoods, linked by small lanes that change their names half way across their paths, a city that is a very loose confederation of neighborhoods of quite different kinds, each with its distinctive internal organization" (Rorty, 1985, p. 116). Rorty views the self as a loose configuration of habits, thoughts, perceptions, motivations and actions, acquired at different stages of development, in the service of different ends. Margolis (1982) proposed that the person can be viewed as two selves, one concerned with selfish benefits and the other with group benefits.

Sidgwick (1893) drew attention to the temporal multiplicity of selves, namely that the "I" of the present moment may be very different from the "I" of the past or of the future, and we might note also that the individual occasionally regresses to the earlier versions of the self. Steedman and Krause (1985) talked of a multifaceted individual having different points of view, whereas others (de Sousa, 1976; Dennett, 1978; Hofstadter & Dennett, 1981; Lycan, 1981) have argued in favor of picturing the self as a hierarchical structure of ever-simpler homunculi. Finally, Elster (1985) proposed what may be a fitting analogy -- the mind as a computer with different programs (software) being loaded and taking control at different times. To extend this analogy, we might suggest for subsubselves, say, the crosstabs routine of SPSSX.

W. R. D. Fairbairn: Object-Relations Theory

Fairbairn (1954) is one of the group of psychoanalysts who have become known as object-relations theorists. Fairbairn proposed that the infant, when faced with a frustrating parent, tries to control this aspect of his environment. In his mind, the infant splits the object into its good and bad aspects and introjects or internalizes the bad aspect. This makes the environment good and the infant bad. Even in extreme cases, abused children tend to see themselves as bad and their parents as good.

Fairbairn proposed also that these internalized aspects, or objects, become dynamic structures that are capable of acting as independent agents within the mind. These structures are located in the ego, and the situation is as if there were a multiplicity of egos at war with one another. Fairbairn called this the endopsychic situation.

Fairbairn also looked at these structures more concretely. He described the libidinal ego, which is that part of the mind that feels needy, attacked, and persecuted; the internal saboteur (or antilibidinal ego, or attacking ego), which is aggressive and attacking especially toward the libidinal ego and resembles the classic Freudian superego; and the central ego, which tries to sever these subsidiary egos and repress them. (The internal saboteur also tries to repress the libidinal ego.)

The goal of psychotherapy is to make the bad objects conscious so that their emotional power can be dissolved. Fairbairn used dream analysis to assist this process. Fairbairn's technique of dream interpretation is similar to that of Perls (1969) in that each element of the dream is assumed to represented an ego structure.

Georges Gurdjieff: A Mystic

Ouspensky (1949) has described the teachings of Gurdjieff, an Armenian mystic, whom he met in the early part of this century in Russia. Many of Gurdjieff's ideas concerning the structure of personality are similar in many ways to the ideas presented here.

Early on Gurdjieff talked of a person containing many different people. He explains, for example, that people cannot keep promises because the "self" that makes the promise is not the same as the "self" that breaks the promise. Gurdjieff suggested that people change selves continually, seldom remaining the same for even 30 minutes. Each of these selves call themselves "I." They each consider themselves masters and do not like to recognize one another. Gurdjieff thought that there was no order among them. Whoever gets the upper hand is master until another seizes power.

> We think that if a man is called Ivan he is always Ivan. Nothing of the kind. Now he is Ivan, in another minute Peter, and a minute later he is Nicholas, Sergius, Matthew, Simon. And all of you think he is Ivan. You know that Ivan cannot do a certain thing. He cannot tell a lie for instance. Then you find he has told a lie and you are surprised he could have done so, and, indeed, Ivan cannot lie; it is Nicholas who lied..... You will be astonished when you realize what a multitude of these Ivans and Nicholases live in one man. (Ouspensky, 1949, p. 53)

These selves have separate minds, entirely independent of one another with separate functions and spheres in which they manifest themselves. These selves are mutually exclusive and incompatible. Thus, the whole never expresses itself, although each individual "I" calls itself by the name of the whole and acts in the name of the whole. One solution is for the many I's to elect a leader who can keep the other I's in their place and make each function at the appropriate time. The ultimate solution for Gurdjieff was for the person to develop a true master, a higher self who can control all of the lesser selves.

The I's are created by experiences and can be affected by external circumstances. Different situations call forth different I's. Thus, Gurdjieff's psychological perspective encompasses learning theory and situationism. These many I's create many contradictions and are in constant conflict. If we were to feel all of these contradictions in one instant, we would feel what we really are, but we would also feel mad. If we cannot destroy the contradictions, we create buffers so that we cease to feel the contradictions. Buffers lessen shocks, but buffers also prevent us from waking up to the path to higher levels of consciousness where there is but a single and permanent "I." Gurdjieff also drew a distinction between the self we present to others and the real self we are.

Later in his description of the path to higher levels of consciousness, Ouspensky describes the task of learning to observe oneself. While behaving, you must try to observe and remember yourself behaving. Self-observation is observation of the mask (c.f., Jung's concept of the persona), the part we unconsciously play and that we cannot stop playing. This division of attention (toward the outside world and toward yourself attending to the outside world) suggests another division of the mind into selves. The self that we really are is essence, whereas the self that we have become because of external influences is our personality. (In Chapter 3, these subselves are called the real self and the façade self.) Infants have only essence, but education immediately creates the personality. Since our essence is often suppressed, it often proves to be on the level of a small child. Once the individual decides to move toward higher levels of functioning, the essence must be developed. A person's real "I" can be developed only from his essence.

Gurdjieff also phrased his ideas in terms of roles. Each person has a definite repertoire of roles that he or she plays in most circumstances. The repertoire of roles is limited to no more than five or six: one or two for family, one or two for work, one for social friends, and one for intellectual friends. When we are in a role, we are fully identified with the role. Without a role we feel undressed. (The proposition that we have five or six roles matches the number of selves proposed by other theorists, as discussed later in Chapter 4.)

Note that there is an inconsistency in Gurdjieff's thinking between the multitude of I's that change from moment to moment and the limited number of roles. This inconsistency can perhaps be resolved by reducing the number of I's and viewing them as having more than a momentary existence.

Mardi Horowitz: States of Mind

Horowitz (1988) proposed the concept of a state of mind. A state of mind is a relatively coherent pattern, a composite of diverse forms of experience and expression that appear almost simultaneously. These states of mind are accompanied by characteristic expressive behaviors (such as the pace or tone of the voice and facial expressions).

Horowitz categorized these states of mind for the degree to which emotions and impulses were controlled: undermodulated, well-modulated, or overmodulated. Horowitz also suggested that one particular state of mind could sometimes try to co-exist with another, a notion that resembles Angyal's concept of the pressure one subsystem can exert on another in its effort to take control of the mind.

Horowitz suggested naming these states of mind so that they can be discussed with the client in psychotherapy and observed by the client when alone. This naming helps the client control the states, because the client can observe his or her mind moving from one state to another.

J. M. M. Mair: A Community of Selves

Mair (1977), a psychologist, has suggested that, rather than viewing the mind as an individual unit, we can consider the mind to a be a "community of selves." The expressions "to be of two minds" about an issue and "to do battle with ourselves" suggest that we sometimes talk and act as if we were two people rather than one. Gestalt therapy (Perls, Hefferline, & Goodman, 1951) includes exercises to enable us to explore these multiple selves.

Mair suggested that it is useful in psychotherapy to encourage people to conceptualize their mind as a community of selves, some of which may be persistent whereas others are transient, some of which are isolates whereas others work as a team, some who appear on many occasions whereas others appear only rarely, and some of which are powerful whereas others are submissive.

Mair gave three clinical examples of individuals who were readily able to conceptualize their minds as a community of selves. One man used a political framework, viewing his mind as made up of a cabinet of ministers in a government. Another used the notion of political factions, whereas the third used the notion of a troupe of actors. The range of analogies used suggests that we may find useful concepts for understanding the mind from politics, group processes, diplomacy, debate, propaganda, industrial organizations, labor relations, international trade, law, theater, literature, arts, or science.

Mair stressed that he considered this to be a metaphor. Our minds sometimes behave as if they were communities of selves. He shrank from postulating that they are communities of selves.

Marvin Minsky: Agencies of the Mind

Minsky (1986), cofounder of the artificial intelligence laboratory at MIT, proposed that there are agencies of the mind, by which he means any and all psychological processes. Although he grants that a view of the mind as made up of many selves may be valid, he suggests that this may be a myth that we construct.

However, when introducing the concept of agencies (a broad term that includes selves as one type of agency), Minsky suggested several important questions to ask about agencies:

How do agents work?
What are they made of?
How do they communicate?
Where do the first agents come from?
Are we all born with the same agents?
How to make new agents and change old ones?
What are the most important kinds of agents?
What happens when agents disagree?
How could networks of agents want or wish?
How can groups of agents do what separate agents cannot do?
What gives them unity or responsibility?
How could they understand anything?
How could they have feelings and emotions?
How could they be conscious or self-aware?

Not all of these questions, of course, apply to subselves. But the questions of origins, heredity, learning, character, authority, and competence are pertinent to subselves.

James Ogilvy: A Multiplicity of Selves

Ogilvy (1977), a philosopher, has criticized two ideal organizations of the mind. First, he argued against the notion that a single unified self exists. Second, he argued against the rationale of theories in which a multiplicity of selves are organized as a social hierarchy with a single powerful self that rules the mind. Ogilvy advocated a theory in which a multiplicity of selves have a decentralized organization.

For Ogilvy, a multiplicity of selves, a pluralized pantheon of selves, as opposed to a single monotheistic ego leads to freedom. (He saw the least free person as one who has a single, highly predictable personality. Predictability, in his view, signifies lack of freedom.) Each self is a source of differing interpretations of the world, based on differing interpretive schemes.

These intrapersonal selves have different personalities. The person is the result of mediation among this collection of individual, relatively autonomous intrapersonal selves. The goal is to prevent any one of these selves from taking control, that is, acting as a monarch or single administrator. Ogilvy saw the ideal as the avoidance of a hierarchical organization of the selves. Instead, a heterarchical organization (McCulloch, 1965), illustrated by the coordination and integration of the different parts of the body, should prevail. Heterarchy does not lead to anarchy. The body, incidentally, is not simply a good analogy for the mind - it is one of the selves.

Ogilvy asked whether the subselves have still further selves and so on, ad infinitum, but decided that they did not. However, the different selves may all have individual ego-ideals, needs, personality traits, and so forth. For Ogilvy, the intrapersonal selves are projected onto mythic figures such as gods, and in turn, the intrapersonal selves are formed from introjected elements from past projections. Thus, we can expect certain commonalities in the intrapersonal selves of different people.

A weaker version of this model describes a person's behavior as the result of a succession of separate identities (or roles, or masks) that are assumed. Ogilvy preferred viewing the selves as working together, much as a group does to achieve a final product (behavior). Individual differences result from the different evolution of the multiple selves and their differing organization.

Sampson (1983), too, has argued for the usefulness of a multicentered self, as opposed to the integrated self proposed by some developmental psychologists, such as Erik Erikson (1968) and Jane Loevinger (1977).

John Rowan: Subpersonalities

Rowan's (1990) preference is for the term subpersonality, and he defines it as "a semi-permanent and semi-autonomous region of the personality capable of acting as a person" (p. 8). Rowan noted that it is necessary, on the one hand, to reify subpersonalities, but on the other hand, to remember that we are not talking about things but about processes that are fluid and in change.

In discussing the origin of subpersonalities, Rowan suggested that roles could bring out accompanying subpersonalities. Internal conflicts, in which two or more sides argue within us also can lead to the formation of subpersonalities. Our bodies can also participate in these conflicts and act antagonistically to our mind.

Thus, the body, or parts of the body, can also be regarded as subpersonalities. Identification with heroes or heroines can sometimes lead to the person taking on the identity of the hero. Subpersonalities can also derive from the Freudian personal unconscious and the Jungian collective unconscious.

In a simple study of subpersonalities, Rowan asked the members of a group he led to describe their subpersonalities. At the first meeting, the number described ranged from 0 to 18 with a mean of 6.5. In later discussions, occasional participants did not seem to have any limit on the number of possible subpersonalities. Other participants could describe subpersonalities from earlier stages of development but felt that those were fading and no longer important. Rowan felt that 4 to 8 was the normal range. Some participants felt comfortable giving names or labels to their subpersonalities, whereas others did not.

The next question addressed by Rowan was whether some subpersonalities might be held in common by many people. Answering this question is by no means easy. Classic theories of personality and psychotherapy provide abstract labels for subpersonalities held in common, such as Perls's (1969) top dog/bottom dog or Berne's (1961) Parent, Adult, and Child ego states. But there may also be more concrete subpersonalities held in common. An analogy here is provided by Steiner's (1974) discussion of scripts in transactional analysis. As well as the abstract scripts of no mind (crazy), no love (depression), and no pleasure (drug abuse), Steiner also described specific scripts such as playboy, jock, and the woman behind the man. Allison and Schwartz (1980) classified subpersonalities into persecutors, rescuers, and internal self-helpers. Rowan himself did not propose a classification of subpersonalities.

Clients in psychotherapy can profitably use the concept of subpersonalities. Clients, if they like this conceptualization, must first identify and accept their subpersonalities. Rowan, following Assagoli (1975), suggests that the next stages are coordination, integration, and synthesis. However, since each subpersonality is an expression of ourselves and need not be harmful (unless they control us), synthesis may not be necessary.

Rowan did propose a developmental sequence for subpersonalities. The infant begins as one unified whole. As Rogers (1981) suggested, the child then differentiates between the part approved of by the parents and the part they disapprove of. The OK regions and the not-OK regions then split into subregions as the child matures, and then the childhood regions, especially the not-OK regions, may become closed off (repressed) under the societal (and parental) pressure. Following Jung (Progoff, 1973), Rowan believes that one or more persona and a shadow develop, as well as a patripsych, a concept borrowed from Southgate and Randall (1978), who define it as an internal constellation of patriarchal patterns -- attitudes, ideas, and feelings that develop in relation to authority and control and that are internalized from the culture in which we live. Because the real self is closed off, the person typically feels hollow. There is no center, and the person must rely on the persona developed to deal with others. At this point psychotherapy can be helpful.

Rowan urged research into such issues as the number, type, and common qualities of the subpersonalities held by people and their structure (egalitarian or hierarchical, communes or committees, etc.). He also put forward several propositions based on the principles of group dynamics, in which the term group member is replaced by subpersonality.

1. Better decisions are made by bringing out and exploring the subpersonalities and by integrating, rather than allowing one subpersonality to dominate, and by making compromises.
2. It is useful to develop one subpersonality to be a trained observer and to give feedback to the group of subpersonalities on the style in which they relate to one another.
3. Disturbances in the interactions and conflict should be given priority for exploration and should not be ignored.
4. Different situations call for different types of leaders, and so each subpersonality may have usefulness for some problems. The goal is to use the subpersonalities rather than be used by them.
5. The subpersonalities will change as they interact more and trust one another more.
6. No one subpersonality can represent or speak for the whole group.

James Vargiu

Vargiu (1974) proposed that semi-autonomous subpersonalities exist in the mind and, when any one expresses itself, lead us to play the corresponding role. We choose which subpersonality we want to express at each moment, which raises the question as to who is the subself that chooses. As a psychotherapist, the goal of therapy is to help the client to become aware of these subpersonalites, get to know them and then regulate and direct their expression. The subpersonalities must be in harmony rather than conflict, and Vargiu achieved this during psychotherapy with his clients in stages – recognition, acceptance, coordination, integration and synthesis.

PERSONAL USE OF THE CONCEPT

The concept of subselves is one which people find easy to use. For example, in the set of films in which a client Gloria is interviewed by Carl Rogers, Frederick Perls, and Albert Ellis (Shostrom, 1965), the metaphor of subselves is present in all interviews.

With Carl Rogers, Gloria talks of her "shady side" and her "ornery devilish side." She also talks of splits in her self. "I want to approve of me always, but my actions won't let me," to which Rogers comments that "It sounds as if your actions are kind of outside of you....It sounds like a triangle, doesn't it? You feel that I or other therapists in general or other people say 'It's all right, natural enough. Go ahead.' I guess you feel your body sort of lines up on that side of the picture, but something in you says, 'But I don't like it that way unless it's really right.'" We seem to have a part of Gloria that passes judgment on another part. She has a body and actions that do one thing, and a part of her mind that argues for an alternative course of action.

With Perls, Gloria exhibits the two polarities of her existence -- the mother, treating others as if they were her children, afraid to be close, and at the other extreme, the little girl, hiding in a corner, waiting to be rescued, but willing to be close. With Ellis, Gloria again refers to parts of herself. She fears showing "stinky part of me" to others, and Ellis tells that she is taking a part of herself and acting as if was the total self. He tells her that she must accept herself with the defective part.

Finally, in the summary interview with Everett Shostrom, Gloria says that she felt her more lovable, caring self with Rogers, but that he would make it hard for her spitfire self to come out. Shostrom comments that she "felt your feeling self with Dr. Rogers, your fighting self with Dr. Perls" and she finishes for him "and my thinking self with Dr. Ellis." Rather than selves, Gloria sometimes refers to "sides," but Shostrom moves to using the notion of subselves to describe Gloria's experiences with the three therapists.

IS A MULTIPLE SELF UNIVERSAL?

Corollary 1a: Not Every Individual Has a Multiple Self

Frick (1993), who preferred the term "the fractured self" or "partial identity," asked whether everyone has a multiple self? Frick suggested that only neurotics have multiple selves, not mature and integrated people. He proposed that the level of integration parallels the level of self-awareness. Subselves are associated with low or distorted levels of awareness. Despite Frick's negative view of the concept of subselves, which I do not accept, his views lead to the proposition that not everyone may have a mind made up of multiple selves.

This raises the question, therefore, of what are the differences between those whose mind can be conceptualized as a multiple self and those whose mind can be conceptualized as a unified self, an issue open to clinical investigation in the future.

IS A MULTIPLE SELF HEALTHY OR PATHOLOGICAL?

Corollary 1b: Having a Unified Self or a Multiple Self Has No Bearing on the Individual's Psychological Health

Some theorists (such as Gergen, 1971) argue that greater pluralism is associated with greater psychological well-being, while others (such as Rogers, 1959) propose that greater unity is associated with greater psychological well-being. Frick (1993) saw a multiple self as an index of psychological disturbance, while Bogart (1994) argued that subselves (which he called personas) can be active players in our efforts to be fully functioning or self-actualized. Clearly, views on the health versus pathology of the unified and multiple self are varied, and the issue can be explored in future research. At the present time, therefore, Corollary 1b is formulated to take a neutral position on the issue. This issue is discussed in greater depth in Chapter 5.

DISCUSSION

Ewing (1990) has argued that the notion that individuals have a unified, whole self, is an illusion, particularly strong in the Western world. As Geertz (1984) has said:

> The Western conception of the person as bounded, unique, more or less integrated motivational and cognitive universe, a dynamic center of awareness, emotion, judgment, and action organized into a distinctive whole and set contrastively both against other such wholes and against its social and

natural background, is, however incorrigible it may seem to us, a rather peculiar idea within the context of the world's cultures. (p. 126)

This illusion of wholeness is created by defense mechanisms, the psychological processes of condensation, displacement, transference and identification, which "create an illusory sense of wholeness and personal continuity out of what are actually inconsistent self-experiences (Ewing, 1990, p. 266). In contrast, cultural anthropologists, making what psychologists would call clinical observations of indigenous peoples in their natural settings, are aware of the varieties of subselves that appear in different contexts, or social settings.

Despite this, Baumeister (1998) stated: "The multiplicity of selfhood is a metaphor. The unity of selfhood is a defining fact" (p. 682). Since Baumeister present no facts to back up his assertion, it could just as appropriately be asserted that the unity of the self is a metaphor while the multiplicity of the self is a fact. In contrast, Corollary 1a of the present theory has granted that some people have a single self while others have a multiple self. It is not crucial, but it is of some importance, that psychological theories match people's experience. Although the present author is convinced of his continued existence as a single individual, he is also quite sure that he has different, subjectively-experienced subselves.

There are many sources from which additional propositions and corollaries about subselves might be identified. Role theory provides such concepts as a role set (a collection of roles), formal and informal roles (such as "professor" and "scapegoat" in the family system), role conflict and role strain (Merton, 1968), role distance in which the individual resists the role and purposely gives inauthentic performances (Goffman, 1961) and role merger, that is, the degree to which individuals see themselves as defined primarily through one of the roles they play (Turner, 1978). It may be important, however, to clarify the distinctions between (or relationships among) the concepts of subselves, identities (especially as defined by Deaux [1991][1]) and roles. Other sources of propositions and corollaries may come from analogies with group dynamics and family therapy. The following chapters will present a series of further propositions and corollaries derived from these diverse sources.

---

[1] "…..membership in recognizable social groups……personal characteristics…[and] attributes of personality shared with a large number of other people" (Deaux, 1991, p. 78). Examples are professor, spouse, friend, woman, Roman Catholic, Hispanic, etc.

Chapter 2

EXECUTIVE POWER

> Sometimes it was as if I were two different people: the one who thought things and the one who said and did things. I couldn't for the life of me, bring the two together. I don't know what I thought might happen if I did, but whatever it was, it scared me. Scared me enough to keep a wall up.
> Mama called it my shade.
>
> (Carol Burnett, 1986, p. 134)

In discussions of subselves, or the variations on this theme, there is often the proposal that one subself is in control of the mind at any one point in time. In Berne's Transactional Analysis, the ego state that has control of the mind is said to have executive power and the other ego-states are said to be decommissioned. In Angyal's theory, one subsystem may tend toward hegemony and take over control of the mind. In George Kelly's (1955) theory of personal constructs, the individual may have two or more sets of constructs that are incompatible with one another. While the mind operates on one set of constructs, the other set is said to be suspended.

The following postulate and corollary, therefore, seems to be reasonable.

POSTULATE 2: At any point in time, one subself is in control of the mind. It may be said to have executive power.

COROLLARY 2a: When one subself has executive power, the other subselves are said to be suspended.

When one subself has executive power, what is the role of the other subselves? Are they idle, ignorant as to what psychological processes are occurring in the subself that has executive power? Alternatively are they monitoring what is occurring in the subself that has executive power, and even perhaps intruding thoughts into the individual's consciousness? This leads to a second corollary.

COROLLARY 2b: When one subself has executive power, some of the other subselves may be monitoring what is being processed by the executive subself, but others may not. Clinical investigation of the individual is necessary to determine which subselves are monitoring the executive subself and which are not.

Clinical investigation is necessary to determine whether a particular individual has subselves that monitor the executive subself, which subselves do monitor and which do not, and also what are the personality correlates and developmental antecedents of the options here. In addition, some suspended subselves may become dissociated (see Chapter 7) and others may become unconscious. Again, clinical investigation is required to identify these phenomena in individuals.

It is of clinical interest here to distinguish between subselves that have unconscious elements along with conscious elements and subselves that are completely unconscious. Jung proposed the existence of complexes (Jung's term for what I call subselves) whose elements were either totally unconscious (complexes such as the shadow and animus/anima) or totally conscious (such as the persona). This has always seemed to me to be too rigid. Some subselves could have both conscious and unconscious elements.

Carl Jung proposed that two attitudes (extraversion versus introversion) and four functions (sensing versus intuition and thinking versus feeling) characterized the complexes. In a discussion of the possible types that result from this, Jung, in an interview with Richard Evans (1981), described the introverted intuitive type as a person who might well monitor their psychological processes in the way described here. Jung gave the example of a young patient who told him, correctly, that she would need only twelve sessions and who described her problem, metaphorically, as having a black snake in her abdomen. During the sessions, the snake rose higher until, during her final session, she told Jung that the snake had come out of her mouth and that it was golden. Indicative of her introversion (which for Jung meant focusing more on internal stimuli and sensations than on external stimuli), one of the woman's symptoms was that she could not hear her footsteps. Furthermore, while she was in psychotherapy with Jung, she had stayed in a hotel which, unbeknownst to her, was a brothel.

We might propose, therefore, that introverted intuitive types might be more likely to report more than one subself, and to have subselves that monitor the activity of the other subselves. An empirical test of this hypothesis would require the use of a test to measure these Jungian dimensions. Lester (1992) asked 44 undergraduates how many subselves they had using the following paragraph:

> Almost all people feel that there are different sides to their personality. We have different roles or different selves depending on the situation or on our mood. I want you to take some time to think about your different selves. How many can you identify and what are their characteristics? Give each a name/title and describe it in three or four words.

The students described an average of 3.5 subselves with a standard deviation of 1.3. The students were given a psychological test devised by Eysenck, Eysenck and Barrett (1985) to measure their level of extraversion, neuroticism and psychoticism. Students high in both extraversion and neuroticism reported more subselves than other students (4.6 versus 3.2), a difference in a direction opposite to that predicted above. It should be noted that Eysenck's test of extraversion assesses sociability and impulsivity, whereas the Jungian concept of extraversion involves paying more attention and giving more weight to external stimuli than to internal stimuli, a very different meaning for the concept. However, this example does illustrate the type of research that can be conducted on subself theory.

We will see later in Chapter 6, that some psychotherapists endeavor to create subselves that function as "recording secretaries" and as mediators in conflict between subselves. This implies, therefore, that some subselves are monitoring the activity of other subselves.

COROLLARY 2c: A subself may have executive power for anywhere from seconds to hours or longer.

When we think of subselves as roles, then it seems reasonable to propose that an individual may set in one subself for long periods of time. If a person is taking care of their child, then the person may set in the role of parent for hours at a time. Subselves that are associated with moods, such as the depressed subself and the happy subself, may also have executive control for hours, days and even longer periods of time in pathological conditions.

However, we are also aware of having internal dialogues with ourselves. In Gestalt Therapy, Perls brought this out in his "hot seat" technique in which he had the client create a dialogue between the top dog and the bottom dog (the nagger and the nagged) or between a quiescent left hand and an expressive, gesturing right hand. Progroff (1974) in his Intensive Journal Workshop, has a number of exercises in which the participant creates (and writes down in a journal) dialogues – between the mind and the body (as well as dialogues between the individual and God, or between the individual and his or her work). Both of these examples can be construed as allowing and encouraging two subselves to have a dialogue or conversation with each other.

It appears, then, that, in some situations, it is appropriate for subselves to have executive power for long periods of time (such as when it is necessary to set in a role for hours, for example, when a professor is lecturing in class or when a student is sitting in class). However, in other situations, it may be useful to have the subselves operate as a group, creating internal dialogues, such as when we are making decisions about important issues for ourselves.

COROLLARY 2d: Selfhood is whichever subself has executive power at the time.

Those psychologists who believe that there is only one self find the notion that individuals have multiple selves (subselves) upsetting because they ask, if we have many subselves, how can we have a stable sense of self over time? How do we recognize that the "me" today is the same person as the "me" yesterday, last month and last year? Selfhood is thought to be unchanging and unchangeable.

Systems theorists would be surprised by this. Open systems are always changing, and yet they remain as stable objects. The water in a river is changing continuously, yet the river persists as an entity. The physical body I have today is nothing like the body I had forty years ago, and yet it still me.

Some personality theorists categorize theories of personality into three of four main types, and a common grouping comprises those theories whose main concept is that of two opposing forces (Maddi, 1972). Classic psychoanalytic theory proposed two instincts, life and death (or eros and thanatos), that oppose each other. Andras Angyal proposed two trends, toward autonomy (seeking the satisfaction of my personal needs) and homonomy (seeking to integrate with family, cultures, nature and God). Personality theorists have no problem in admitting that individuals have internal conflicts between opposed desires, attitudes and values.

If individuals have developed an observing self, then their sense of self also has a component of awareness that they have many subselves, and that who they are changes from time to time. The self changes but remains "me."

This leads us to the next issue, Mischel's critique of intrapsychic theories of personality.

MISCHELS' SITUATIONAL CRITIQUE OF INTRAPSYCHIC THEORIES OF PERSONALITY

The major intrapsychic theories of personality, like the theory presented in this book, assume that individual differences between people exist because people differ in their psychodynamic processes or personality traits. Mischel (1968) argued that assumption was incorrect. Instead, Mischel argued that people behaved differently because of the different situations that they found themselves in and because of their different histories of learning.

Mischel's Argument

The evidence that Mischel reviewed to support his view came from studies that indicated that people did not behavior consistently across different situations. For example, Mischel and Peake (1982) found no consistency in the friendliness or consciousness of students in different situations. The strength of the associations between a "trait" measured in different situations was typically around 0.3 which means that the association accounts for about ten percent of the variance in behavioral measures.

Cloninger (2000) noted that lay persons intuitively think of people as behaving consistently, yet research does not support this, and even anecdotal evidence contradicts the notion that people behave consistently. Cloninger noted that people who are honest in the classroom may cheat on taxes; children who wait patiently when their parents are present may act impulsively when their parents are no longer present. As Mischel (1968) put it:

> In spite of methodological reservations, however, it is evident that the behaviors which are often construed as stable personality trait indicators are highly specific and depend on the details of the evoking situations and the response mode employed to measure them. (p. 37)

> Although it is evident that persons are the source from which human responses are evoked, it is the situational stimuli that evoke them, and it is changes in the conditions that alter them. (p. 296)

There were many critiques of Mischel's argument (e.g., Epstein, 1983) and rebuttals by Mischel (e.g., Mischle & Peake, 1983). Of course, extreme positions are useful in establishing a scholar's visibility and fame, but they are typically incorrect. The "truth" is usually an intermediate position which synthesas the opposing, extreme views. Today, therefore, we can assert that behavior in both a function of intrapsychic processes *and* situational determinants.

Let us look at some of the arguments made against Mischel's hypothesis. It may be that our measurement techniques are flawed. A groups of students may be given a test of extraversion-introversion and then observed during a class discussion and rated by an observer who does not know their psychological test scores on how extraverted they are behaviorally. If the correlation is low, this may throw doubt on the consistency of behavior, but it may also throw doubt on the validity of the measures, both the psychological test and the behavioral measure.

It is interesting to note in this respect that, back in the 1940s, personality theorists and researchers such as Sheldon (1942), who proposed a physiological theory of personality, would have been horrified at such simplistic measures of personality and behavior. They collected dossiers of psychological test scores and behavioral measures obtained from groups of students over a period of four years – during their whole undergraduate experience. Only then, after a long period of observation and study, did they think that accurate judgments could be made about the personality of individuals.

One solution to the dilemma of the unreliability of some of the measures used in current research is to aggregate data. Epstein (1979) showed that the ratings by students of their mood (positive or negative) on individual days showed very little consistency. However, if the aggregate of their self-ratings on odd days was compared to their aggregate ratings on even days, there was high consistency. But of course, such aggregation eliminates and ignores the subtle nuances of human behavior – in this case the day-to-day variability of human behavior.

On the other hand, a situational approach also ignores the subtle nuances of human behavior. In my classes, I illustrate this by asking students in the front row of the class whether they typically sit in the front row - almost all say that they do; and the same is true for the students in the back of the class. Yet they are all in the same situation. Situational theorists would argue that the history of rewards and punishments of the students, their antecedent learning experiences, determine this difference in behavior (sitting in the front of the class or at the back). However, the researcher has no way of assessing the history of rewards and punishments of the students. Indeed most people cannot recall their history of rewards and punishments and, for many, they were not aware of these contingencies when they occurred. The researcher can, however, measure a personality trait and observe a behavior in the current situation.

The Consistency of Behavior Over Time

Another argument often used to argue against the existence of stable personality traits and psychodynamic processes is the fact that people's behavior and personality change over time. From a situational perspective, obviously the situations are very different at different points in an individual's life. Furthermore, the individual is subjected to a changing pattern of rewards and punishments over a lifetime which may also change personality and behaviors.

However, intrapsychic theories do not discount the impact of learning. Indeed, the most powerful intrapsychic theory of personality, psychoanalytic theory, proposes detailed accounts of the way in which experiences shape the particular psychodynamic process that determine an individual's behavior.

COROLLARY 2e: The existence of subselves accounts for the occasional inconsistency in the behavior of individuals. The behavior of an individual may differ when each subself has executive power.

The present multiple self theory of personality easily accounts for the inconsistency of people's behavior. The apparent inconsistencies in an individual's behavior in two situations may be the result of different subselves having executive power in the different situations. In the example above of people behaving honestly in the classroom setting, but cheating on their taxes, it is clear that the people have different subselves with executive power in the two situations or, if one prefers a role terminology, the people are in different roles in the two situations.

Reluctant though I may be to give others credit for these ideas, even Mischel (1968) alluded to this possibility.

> Temporal stability is also enhanced when individuals categorize themselves with relatively permanent trait labels (smart, dumb, attractive, excessively dependent).....The labels and categories that people attribute to themselves also may exert stabilizing effects on their own subsequent behavior and on their reactions to themselves.....Sociologists have noted repeatedly that societal role and role labels convey stable expectations and contingencies that serve to stabilizer the behavior of the individual who holds that role.....The effects are especially strong when the role labels are permanent. This seen, for example, in the development of relatively stable sex roles and of fairly enduring self-concepts about one's masculine or feminine attributes.....(pp. 284-285)

It appears, therefore, that the behavior of an individual when a particular subself has executive power may be quite consistent but, when another subself takes over executive power, then the individual's behavior may change dramatically.

CONFLICTING DESIRES

Often people find themselves with two (or more) conflicting desires. You want to work on that project, but you also want to watch that program on television. You love your spouse and want to remain faithful, but that individual you are having a drink with over lunch is so tempting.

Some theories of personality make such conflicts the core feature of their theory. Maddi (1972) classified theories of personality into three types. *Fulfillment* theories assume that one great force drives the person, and they view life as a progressively greater expression of this force. Maddi places the theories of Carl Rogers, Abraham Maslow, Alfred Adler, Gordon Allport, Erich Fromm and the existential psychologists in this category. *Consistency* theories emphasize feedback from the external world and whether it is or is not consistent with what was expected. Maddi placed the theories of George Kelly, David McClelland and Leon Festinger here.

Maddi's third category of theories of personality was *conflict* theories. Maddi suggested that there were two types of conflict theories: (i) psychosocial in which the conflict is between the individual and interpersonal/social forces, and (ii) intrapsychic in which both forces originate within the individual. Maddi placed the theories of Sigmund Freud, Henry Murray and Harry Stack Sullivan in the psychosocial group, and the theories of Otto Rank, Andras Angyal, David Bakan and Carl Jung in the intrapsychic group.

I like Maddi's classification scheme, but I disagree strongly with his placement of the theories into the scheme. Despite this, Maddi's conflict category is relevant for the present theory. I view the theories of Freud, Angyal and Jung as the major conflict theories of personality.

Sigmund Freud, in his later version of psychoanalytic theory, proposed two competing forces. The life instinct, as he named it, or Eros, fueled by an energy which he named libido, is the force that drives us to acquire, conquer, expand, grow – all of the desires for which gratification would bring us pleasure. The death instinct, or Thanatos, fueled by an energy named destrudo, is self-destructive, driving us to thwart our growth, harm ourselves, even to the point of seeking death.[2]

Andras Angyal also proposed two forces that motivate human behavior. The trend toward autonomy covers those drives in which we grow, expand and prosper at the expense of the environment. This manifests itself as the desire to achieve, the desire to dominate, the need to defend our integrity and maintain our inviolacy, the drive to acquire possessions, and curiosity. But we also have a trend toward homonomy in which we strive to integrate with the environment – to have a family, discover our genealogical roots so that we feel a continuity with previous generations, be part of social group, a community and a culture, to become one with nature or to become one with God. Some acts, like making love to someone we love, satisfies both trends. We communicate with our lover, seek to give them pleasure and strengthen the bond between us, but we also satisfy our sexual desire to have an orgasm.

For Jung, every complex (which in the present theory would be called a subself) in the conscious mind is balanced by a complex in the unconscious mind. The pairs of complexes are balanced on three dimensions, one attitude and two functions. The attitude can be extraverted (relying more on information from the external world) versus introverted (relying more on internally-generated information). The first function is thinking versus feeling, that is, whether decisions are based primarily upon cognitive (thought) processes or on emotions. The second function is sensing versus intuition, that is, whether decisions are based on what stimuli are sensed (and perceived) or whether decisions are based on intuition (which Jung saw as governed more by unconscious processes). Thus, a conscious complex which, for example, can be characterized as extraverted, thinking and sensing will be balanced by an unconscious complex that is introverted, feeling and intuitive. Thus, complexes occur in pairs with opposed attitudes and functions.

Consider, then, individuals torn by two conflicting desires or by two major forces operating within their minds. It may be that this could be viewed as a unified self which possesses two conflicting desires or forces. A much better conceptualization is of two subselves, each motivated by one of the pair of desires or forces. Let us take the example of the conflict between working on a scholarly project and relaxing by watching television. It is reasonable to construe this as two subselves seeking executive power. The organization of the mind, and the resulting behavior (demeanor, tone of voice, etc.), will be very different in the two states. For example, when the working subself is in control, the person may be

---

[2] Modern psychological theories no longer propose sources of "energy" (Hebb, 1949; Lester, 1995).

focused, oblivious to all external stimulation, and able to concentrate for hours. (Using Jung's dimensions, this subself may be introverted and thinking.) In contrast, when the relaxation subself takes over, the individual may be focused on external stimulation (the television and the behavior of others in the room) and very emotional (extraverted and feeling).

Considering the more abstract perspective, two major forces operating in our life, most individuals have engaged in sexual activity when the primary driving force was the trend toward autonomy (or the physiological need for sexual release to conceptualize this in Maslow's hierarchy of needs), and also when the primary force was the trend toward homonomy, that is, the desire to merge with someone else in the act of love and communicate that love to that person. These two subselves are very differently organized, and the organizations affect every aspect of the behaviors.

These considerations, therefore, lead to a new corollary:

Corollary 2f: Subselves can account for the co-existence of two conflicting desires or forces in the mind.

Chapter 3

THE VARIETIES OF SUBSELVES

There will be time, there will be time
To prepare a face to meet the faces that you meet;

T. S. Eliot (The love song of J. Alfred Prufrock)

Richards (1990) argued that the schemes for categorizing a person's subselves are unlimited. There may be no common set of labels, but rather individuals may have their own set of labels. This is reminiscent of George Kelly's Theory of Personal Constructs (Kelly, 1955), in which there are no common constructs found in all people, but rather a unique set of constructs found in each individual.

However, other theorists have argued that the subselves of different people do have similar properties. For example, Eric Berne (1961) proposed that every individual has three ego states: Parent, Adult and Child (see Chapter 1). The contents of each person's Child ego state, for example, may be different, but everyone has a Child ego state of some kind.

There have been many proposals for the types of subselves that might exist. Some theorists have suggested that there is a core self (Kelly, 1955) and what has been called a social self, pseudo-self, false self or, preferably, *façade self* (Laing, 1969; Rogers, 1959; Wagner, 1971; Winnicott, 1960). It is perhaps not useful to single out only one of the subselves as a core self or to have only one façade self. It seems more reasonable to propose several subselves which are equivalent (although differing in their influence on behavior) as core subselves, and several façade selves in much the same way as a person can have several roles.

POSTULATE 3: There are several possibilities for subselves that are common to all individuals.

THE FAÇADE SELF

COROLLARY 3a: One common set of subselves consists of one or more core selves and one or more façade selves.[3]

Andras Angyal's concept of the pattern of vicarious living, part of his theory of personality, is relevant here. Angyal (1941, 1965) tried to maintain a holistic perspective when he considered disturbed behavior. His terms for healthy and disturbed behavior were biopositive and bionegative, and these adjectives referred to the organization of the mind, not to its contents.

The Gestalt psychologists of the 1930s used a visual analogy. The famous vase/face picture can be seen as a vase or as two faces. As the organization changes from one interpretation to the other, the parts of the picture do not move, but each part performs a different function.

Angyal, like Freud, suggested that trauma early in life is the cause of the rival unhealthy system principle. Angyal considered only neurosis (although R. D. Laing's theory suggests that Angyal's ideas can be extended easily to psychosis – see later in this chapter), and he proposed two patterns for the neurotic system principle.

The Pattern of Vicarious Living

The method of adjustment in the pattern of vicarious living is the systematic repression of one's genuine personality and an attempt to replace it with a substitute personality. This substitute personality has been called the social self or the pseudo-self by other writers, but I will refer to it as the façade self, since it is the self we present to others and by means of which we seek to hide our real self. This strategy leads to symptoms such as feelings of emptiness and vacuousness, a pervasive dissatisfaction with the way we are, and attempts to escape from these feelings by getting signs of approval for our façade self from others.

Why should such a strategy be adopted? Angyal suggested that it was because the person felt unloved and unliked as a child. If children feel unloved by their

---

[3] For a detailed discussion of the façade self see Arkin (1981).

parents, then they typically assume that it is their own fault. Therefore, in order to receive love and approval, they must suppress (and eventually repress) their real selves and become what they think others want them to be. Angyal noted that this was the pattern of disturbance proposed by almost all psychological theorists, and we shall see in the following sections that this seems to be the case.

This pattern leads to hysterical neurosis (now called conversion disorder), the hysterical and histrionic personality and, when negativism is present too, psychopathy (the antisocial personality disorder).

The Pattern of Noncommitment

This pattern results in a person who is confused as to whether the world is basically good and friendly versus bad and hostile. This leads to uncertainty and ambivalence. Are people good and trustworthy or bad and untrustworthy, and how can this confusion be dispelled?

These people express fear and hostility toward a presumably hostile world, seem confused and indecisive, and adopt techniques to dispel the confusion such as obsessions, compulsions, and rituals. If I do this in such a way, then today will be fine. I remember as a child that we believed that the day would go well if we managed to walk to school without stepping on the cracks in the sidewalk paving, a behavior indicative of this pattern.

This pattern arises when children are faced with an inconsistent world. Today Daddy is kind and friendly, but yesterday he was angry. Yesterday, Mommy laughed at what we said, but today she hit us. Other people are unpredictable, and ambiguity comes to characterize every situation that the child faces. This pattern leads to anxiety and a search for ways to dispel the anxiety, frequently resulting in obsessive and compulsive behaviors and, in the extreme, obsessive-compulsive disorder.

Eysenck (1967), coming from biological and learning perspectives, has also concluded that there are two types of neurotic patterns -- hysteric neurosis/psychopathy and dysthymia (Eysenck's term for anxiety disorders). When two theorists, with very different perspectives agree that that there are two patterns, we can be reasonably sure that there are, indeed, two patterns.

Hysterics see the world as depriving them. Their desires remain unfulfilled. They see themselves as unliked and unlikable. Their goal is to gain approval. Obsessive-compulsives see the world as threatening. If they are not careful, they may be destroyed. They feel weak and defenseless. Their aim is to develop skills to ward off enemies.

Hysterics concentrate on the self. They feel empty and worthless. The obsessive-compulsive focuses on the environment, which is potentially threatening. Hysterics highlight the existential issue of life and death since they systematically "kill" (repress) their real selves; obsessive-compulsives highlight the existential issue of good and evil.

Angyal felt that almost all theories of disturbed behavior proposed by other scholars focused on what he called the pattern of vicarious living, and many other theorists have proposed a similar pattern. However, although the essence of these alternative versions of the pattern of vicarious living are similar to Angyal's version, they are often embedded in a different context that may change the connotations of the theory. Furthermore, they often use different terms, terms that some clinicians may prefer over those proposed by Angyal.

Arthur Janov

Arthur Janov (1972), who developed primal scream therapy, has a theory of disturbed behavior that is in some respects similar to psychoanalytic theory. He felt that babies have important psychological and physiological needs that have to be gratified. These needs include being fed, held, stimulated, kept warm, and so forth. These needs are the primal needs. Babies often have their needs ignored because their parents fail to gratify them. Some babies suffer more frustration of their needs than do other babies. If their needs are consistently not gratified, babies learn to block out of their awareness (that is, repress) the emotions that accompany the deprivations. With continued severe deprivation, babies also learn to repress the needs themselves, and they will pursue substitute gratifications instead. Satisfying these substitute needs is seen by Janov as satisfying the primal needs symbolically. This is the essence of neurotic behavior -- the symbolic satisfaction of primal needs. So far, Janov's theory resembles Freud's psychoanalytic theory quite closely.

Janov also focused on the demands that parents place upon their children -- to get good grades, be quiet, be clean, and so forth. The greater the demands imposed upon the child by the parents, the more likely it is that the child's real needs will be unsatisfied. Each time this happens, the child experiences a primal pain, and the needs and their accompanying feelings are denied or suppressed and become repressed (that is, unconscious). These individual primal pains are added to the primal pool.

Typically, some event happens to the child that crystallizes all of these developments for the child - the primal scene. Some event takes place, and the child realizes that there is no hope of being loved for what he or she is. This major primal scene is of course merely one scene in a long sequence of scenes, but it is the one that is remembered and serves to symbolize the whole childhood. The child learns to generalize from this one scene and make predictions about how the parents will behave thereafter. Janov felt that the primal scene, that is, the one crucial for crystallizing the child's experience, usually occurs between the ages of 5 and 7.

After the primal scene, the child typically decides to suppress all of the desires that are incompatible with the parents' goals. Thereafter the child tries to please the parents in the way that the parents appear to want. The child suppresses the real self or true self and builds a shell around himself or herself, a defense system or unreal self. The real self and the unreal self then act in a constant dialectic contradiction, with the unreal self continually preventing the person's real needs from emerging and being fulfilled. This part of Janov's theory is very similar to the pattern of vicarious living described in Angyal's theory of personality.

Janov's theory has several holistic conceptions in it. For example, Janov saw symptoms as hooked into systems. Janov opposed treating only the symptoms of the patient. Rather, the therapist must treat the cause that organizes the symptoms. In fact, Janov noted that symptoms often do not disappear until quite late in the course of primal therapy, after the causes of the symptoms have been thoroughly explored. (Incidentally, Janov felt that symptoms are idiosyncratic solutions to the problem of satisfying the primal needs in a symbolic manner, and so there is no universal symbolism in the symptoms shown by patients.) The holistic aspects of Janov's views are manifest in his belief that "as long as any part of the unreal system is allowed to remain, it will stay vigorous and suppress the real system" (Janov, 1972, p. 413). A patient cannot be merely a little neurotic, then. He is either healthy or neurotic, a conception also found in the theory of personality described by Andras Angyal. A person is not "just being neurotic; neurosis is his being" (Janov, 1972, p. 59).

For Janov, fear is the fear of not being loved. This fear threatens the child's existence and is repressed. Anxiety is the present arousal of this fear. Anxiety may or may not be conscious, but it is always rooted in the primal fear. It may be experienced, but it is rarely accurately focused. Fear relates to the past; anxiety relates to the present. Tension is the muscular concomitant of anxiety. Anxiety is the emotion; tension the movements that accompany it.

Janov divided feelings into genuine ones (those experienced by the true self) and pseudo-feelings (those experienced by the unreal self). Most common feelings, such as guilt, depression, rejection, shame, and pride are pseudo-feelings. For example, pride is experienced when the unreal self is successful.

> Stripped of shame, guilt, rejection and all the other pseudo-feelings, he will understand that the pseudo-feelings are but synonyms for the covered great Primal feelings of being unloved.....The emptied-out neurotic will also learn how few are the feelings of man. (Janov, 1972, p. 74)

Defenses are sets of behavior that automatically block primal (genuine) feelings. They can be involuntary (the typical psychoanalytic defense mechanisms) or voluntary (such as smoking, eating, or drug use). Defense mechanisms can also be classified as tension building (such as knotting your stomach muscles) or tension releasing (such as bed-wetting).

Janov used neurosis as a broad term; or rather he saw neurosis as underlying most of the minor psychiatric disturbances. In a broad sense, neurosis for Janov referred to the whole of the developmental mechanism described so far in this section. Neurosis indicates the ways that defense mechanisms are linked together. Neurosis can, therefore, result in all kinds of symptoms including the traditional neurotic symptoms as well as those of the personality disorders and the psychosomatic disorders.

Janov's theory can be reconceptualized as a mix of Freud's psychoanalytic theory and Angyal's holistic theory, and, in particular, Janov saw what Angyal called the pattern of vicarious living as the prototypical neurotic style.

Sidney Jourard

Sidney Jourard (1971a, 1971b) was concerned with one major issue in his writing, namely, what characteristics do psychologically healthy people have? He stressed a few characteristics of such people.

First, psychologically healthy people do not distort what they experience. They perceive events as they really are. If what they perceive is not in accord with their concepts, then they suspend their concepts. The willingness to suspend concepts and beliefs applies to yourself, to others, and to the world. There is also a willingness to inform and revise concepts with fresh inputs of perception. In contrast, the unhealthy person "chronically conceptualizes the world" and "freezes it in only one of its many possibilities."

This can easily be rephrased using the terms of George Kelly's personal construct theory. The healthy person is obviously building a more effective construct system and is the antithesis of George Kelly's (1955) concept of hostility.[4] The healthy person also is dilated (open to new experiences) rather than constricted. Jourard's view of health and Kelly's view are clearly congruent, at least in this respect.

A second important feature of healthy people is the willingness to disclose themselves, to permit others to know them as they now are. Their aim in disclosing themselves is to be perceived by other people as the person they know themselves to be. Healthy people are authentic. Jourard does limit the conditions under which we actively disclose ourselves. Disclosure is appropriate when we feel it is safe to be known and when we feel that it will be beneficial to be known. (Jourard hints at the possibility that self-disclosure can be inappropriate and motivated by neurotic rather than healthy needs.)

Unhealthy people camouflage their true being, possibly to prevent criticism or rejection, with the result that they are misunderstood by others. They join the "lonely crowd," and more importantly they tend to lose touch with their real selves. Jourard argued that "no man can come to know himself except as an outcome of disclosing himself to another person" (Jourard, 1971a, p. 6). Furthermore, self-disclosure encourages others to disclose themselves. There is reciprocity which, in turn, leads to intimacy.

Pathology is a result, therefore, of less than optimal self-disclosure to others. Indeed it is often an active struggle to avoid becoming known by others. Neurotic and psychotic symptoms are "smoke screens interposed between the patient's real self and the gaze of the onlooker....[They are] devices to avoid becoming known" (Jourard, 1971a, p. 32). Less than optimal self-disclosure leads, in Jourard's view to physical, psychosomatic, and psychological illness.

Psychotherapy was seen by Jourard as involving catharsis, and additionally, self-disclosure and confession. By self-disclosure, patients begin to learn more about their authentic selves. Jourard saw the social system in which we live, the social, political, and economic "facts of life," as requiring that we learn roles. Agencies of social control restrict what we reveal about ourselves to what is deemed sane, legal, and good. Society causes us to repress our authentic self, and this leads to illness. Jourard's view of the repression of our authentic self and its replacement by a socially defined role is identical to Angyal's description of the pattern of vicarious living.

A third component of Jourard's discussion of psychological health concerns the role of optimism versus pessimism, or as he calls it inspiration and dispiration.

---

[4] Hostile people distort or extort data so that it fits their theories of the world.

Dispiriting events are the fertile soil for illness; inspiring events for psychological health. Psychotherapy is seen by Jourard as an inspiring event.

Jourard's views are not sufficiently complex and well-articulated as to merit being called a theory. However, his views can be seen to be congruent with the Angyal's theory.

R. D. Laing

Angyal applied the pattern of vicarious living only to neurotic patterns of behavior. This raises the question of whether it might also apply to psychotic patterns of behavior, or whether instead psychosis requires a different system principle. The ideas of R. D. Laing, a Scottish existential psychiatrist, suggest that the pattern of vicarious living may apply to schizophrenia and that, therefore, one unhealthy system principle will suffice.

The basic concept for Laing was experience, and Laing noted that people are not permitted by their parents, family, and society to have authentic experiences. What is the cause of this alienation from experience and this destruction of the self? Laing focused primarily upon the parents' behaviors toward the child, which he felt destroy most of the infant's potentialities. We are taught what to experience. We learn the right way to behave and the right way to feel. Laing (1969) sometimes used the term ego to refer to the false self that adjusts to an alienated and alienating social reality.

All people adopt a pseudo-self, a false outer self. All you can see of me is not the complete me, or perhaps not the real me. The schizophrenic feels a split between the mind and the body, and usually identifies the self with the mind. Thus, the real self becomes disembodied. To be disembodied means that you have no sense of being biologically alive. Your body is but another object in the world. This disembodied self becomes hyperconscious, forms its own ideations and images, and develops a complex relationship with the body.

The schizophrenic has, therefore, a disembodied real self, which is hidden behind the false self system, and the real self is shut up, isolated and impoverished. Ontological insecurity makes the real self fear engulfment by the identity of others. It even fears being destroyed by others. Thus, the schizophrenic's false self system is erected in order to protect the real self from attack. The schizophrenic does not gain any gratification from the activities of the false self. Hysteric people, in contrast, do gain much gratification from the actions of the false self, although they may deny this.

For the schizophrenic, the inner, disembodied real self hates and fears the false self. To assume an alien identity can be a threat to your own identity. People with catatonia try to strip themselves of all behavior in order to deal with this fear of take-over, and they fall into stupors. Schizophrenics, therefore, have adopted a false self system in order to protect their real self from our observation, but they are then threatened by the presence of the false self system they have erected. Their false self becomes a prison. The false self becomes more extensive, more autonomous, and more dead, unreal, false, and mechanical, while the real self becomes impoverished, empty, dead, and more charged with fear and hatred because it is cut off from communication with the outer world.

Laing describes the inner self in the schizophrenic as follows:

1. Its orientation is a primitive oral one, concerned with the dilemma of sustaining its aliveness, while being terrified to "take in" anything. It becomes parched with thirst, and desolate.
2. It becomes charged with hatred of all that is there. The only way of destroying and of not destroying what is there may be to destroy oneself.
3. The attempt to kill the self may be undertaken intentionally. It is partly defensive (If I'm dead, I can't be killed); partly an attempt to endorse the crushing sense of guilt that oppresses the individual (who has no sense of a right to be alive).
4. The "inner" self itself becomes split and loses its own identity and integrity.
5. It loses its own realness and direct access to realness outside itself.
6. The place of safety of the self becomes a prison. The would-be haven becomes a hell. It ceases even to have the safety of a solitary cell. Its own enclave becomes a torture chamber. The inner self is persecuted within this chamber by split concretized parts of itself or by its own phantoms that have become uncontrollable. (Laing, 1969, pp. 172-173)

The false self system and the inner self can also split into fragments, which leads to intrapsychic chaos. This molecular splitting, even of the sequence of behavior, is common to schizophrenics (whereas, in the hysteric, the splitting is molar -- that is, occurs between subsystems). In occasional cases of psychosis, Laing notes that what appears to have happened is that the false self system has been suddenly stripped away, revealing the ontologically insecure and disembodied inner self.

Laing, like Angyal, described a particular form of psychopathology involving the split between the real inner self and the false self system, much as in Angyal's description of the pattern of vicarious living. Laing added a more complex description of the types of false self systems and real (inner) selves that can arise, in particular, differentiating between those found in the hysteric and those found in the schizophrenic individual. Thus, although Angyal saw the pattern of vicarious living as part of the neurotic system principle, Laing's theorizing suggests that the same pattern can used to explain and describe what is going on in the psychotic individual, which represents an important step forward in our understanding of human behavior, both normal and abnormal.

Carl Rogers

In addition to describing a technique for conducting psychotherapy (called among other things Rogerian therapy, nondirective therapy, client-centered therapy and, most recently, person-centered therapy), Carl Rogers has also described a theory of personality. The most explicit formulation of this theory is found in Rogers (1959).

Rogers suggested that the infant has an inherent tendency toward actualizing its potential, and its behavior is directed toward satisfying this need. If this need is satisfied, the infant experiences pleasure. Rogers noted that the infant is best conceptualized as an organized whole, a gestalt. Furthermore, the infant's perception of the environment is more critical in affecting its behavior than is the environment "as it really is."

Part of the process of actualizing involves differentiation, and soon a portion of the child's experience becomes symbolized in an awareness of being. This awareness may be described, according to Rogers, as self-experience. Eventually, this awareness becomes elaborated into a concept of self.

About this time of development, the child develops a need for positive regard. This need is universal, pervasive, and persistent. Rogers does not have an opinion as to whether the need is innate or learned. When the child interacts with adults, particularly its mother, it begins to search for and be satisfied by love from her. The likelihood of receiving this maternal love eventually becomes more important in determining its behavior than its need to actualize itself.

Soon the child develops a need for positive self-regard, and whether the child feels this positive self-regard will depend to a large extent on whether its parents give it positive regard. Typically, parents set up conditions of worth, that is, they regard the child positively only if certain conditions are met. Their regard for it is said to be conditional. As a result, such a child will have positive self-regard only if it meets these conditions of worth.

In contrast, in the healthiest environment, a child would receive unconditional positive regard. The child would be prized and valued by its parents no matter what it is or what it does. In this case, no conditions of worth would be set up. Rogers felt that this case was hypothetically possible and theoretically important but not found in the real world.

Once conditions of worth are set up, then the child begins to experience discrepancies between the conditions of worth and its actual experiences. When experiences are in accord with its conditions of worth, Rogers felt that the child will accurately perceive and symbolize the experiences. When the experiences are not in accord with the conditions of worth, the child's perception of the experiences may be selective and distorted. This process tends to break down the unity of the organism. Certain experiences tend to threaten the child's self. To maintain its self-concept, the child has to resort to defensive maneuvers. The child's behavior is regulated sometimes by its self and sometimes by elements of experience that are not included in the self. The personality becomes divided. The self is no longer true to itself. For the sake of preserving the positive regard of others, the self has falsified some of the values it has experienced. Rogers notes that this is not a conscious choice, but rather a result of the child's development in the presence of its parents.

The incongruence between the child's self and its experience leads to incongruencies in its behavior, some of which are consistent with its self and some with experiences that have not been assimilated into its self. Experiences that are incongruent with the self and with the conditions of worth are "subceived" as threatening, by which Rogers implied that the perception of threat is not necessarily conscious. The nature of threat is that, were the experience to be perceived accurately, then the conditions of worth would be violated. Then the need for positive self-regard would be frustrated, and the child would feel anxiety.

This leads to neurosis. Neurosis basically involves selectively perceiving - denying to awareness some aspects of your experience and distorting your experience in order to keep your total perception of experience consistent with your conditions of worth. Rogers includes in such maneuvers psychological processes such as rationalization, compensation, fantasy, projection, compulsions, phobias, paranoid behaviors, and catatonic states.

If the incongruence between an experience and the conditions of worth is large, occurs suddenly, and has a high degree of obviousness, then these neurotic defensive coping mechanisms cannot operate successfully. Anxiety will be experienced and a state of disorganization will exist. We would see such an individual undergo an acute psychotic breakdown. The person's behavior will appear to be irrational. Typically, the behavior is consistent with the denied aspects of experience rather than consistent with the self. For example, if people have kept their sexual impulses under rigid control, denying them as an aspect of their self, then during their state of disorganization they may act upon such sexual impulses.

An individual undergoing such a process may take one of two paths. The denied experiences may stay dominant, and the person will defend against an awareness of the self. Alternatively, the self may regain dominance, but it will be a greatly altered self. For example, the self will probably contain the theme that the self is a crazy, unreliable person with no control over its impulses.

Clearly, Rogers has provided a detailed analysis of the pattern of vicarious living as described by Angyal. Rogers has adopted a holistic viewpoint, and he has described the process by which the pattern of vicarious living develops. Rogers has added, however, a detailed examination of this process that clarifies it greatly, and he has added some suggestions as to how psychosis might be incorporated into the framework, something that Angyal did not attempt to do. Over the years, Rogers' terminology has become very popular and is the most commonly used way of describing the pattern of vicarious living.

Edwin Wagner

Edwin Wagner (1971) proposed a distinction in personality that is similar to the ideas reviewed so far in this chapter. Wagner argued that personality can be seen as the result of two psychological structures: a façade self and an introspective self.

The façade self is a hierarchically organized set of attitudes and behavioral tendencies that are acquired early in life and that become automatic. These tendencies constitute our basic contact with reality and are formed at a preverbal level. These tendencies include our perception and automatic reactions to stimuli. The façade self is environmentally programmed (that is, determined by the environment).

The introspective self includes our conscience, motivation, and perseverance and has an evaluative and corrective effect on the façade self. The introspective self develops later in life as we become more cognizant of our behavior and as we establish a self-concept. Our introspective self includes such entities as our fantasies, our ideals, and our life-styles. It is heavily dependent upon our language and verbal processes. The introspective self has an enlarged sense of identity, which is derived initially from our awareness of the operation of the façade self and subsequently expanded to include moral judgments, personal aspirations, lifestyle, conscience, and general philosophical outlook. It is internally programmed (that is, self-generated).

The façade self leads to reactions with little reflection or premeditation. It is focused upon the specific and concrete here and now. It is analytic. The introspective self does not lead to behavior directly (except for fantasy, talking to oneself, and rumination). It leads to behavior only by acting upon the façade self. The introspective self deals with wishes, possibilities, and potentialities. It is synthetic and tends to condense, simplify and organize.

The façade self and the introspective self are structurally distinct, according to Wagner, but functionally interrelated. The direction of influence is from the introspective self to the façade self. The façade self tries to preserve itself as it is by means of coping mechanisms, which are analogous to psychoanalytic defense mechanisms. The most efficient coping mechanisms are intellectualization, routine activities (becoming compulsively preoccupied with environmental activities), socialization (joining groups such as a church or a club), professionalization (identifying with your work), and sexualization (providing proof of one's masculinity or femininity through one's clothes, activities, or attitudes). The less efficient coping mechanisms are repression, dissociation, and denial.

The distinction between these two "selves" is quite similar to that made by Rogers in his distinction between a person's introjected condition of worth and his or her experiences, and to that made by Jourard of the authentic self and the social self. However, the particular phrasing that Wagner uses leads to different implications. For example, the introspective self develops later in life. It is not that the healthy child is made unhealthy by the behavior of its parents and represses its true identity. The introspective self involves a cognitive appraisal that is possible only with maturity. In addition, Wagner has applied his structural analysis to a variety of psychopathological types in a much more complex way than other theorists. Let me give some examples.

The façade self and the introspective self complement each other and reciprocate, but they may conflict. If the introspective self is extensive and strong and the façade self is weak, the result may be paranoid and schizoid types who are richly endowed with fantasy, delusions, and idiosyncratic thinking. The façade self is necessary for reality-oriented behavior. The delusions and disturbed cognitions in the schizoid patient come from the introspective self. Wagner noted that, in the paranoid patient, these cognitions are oversimplifications.

Other variants of schizoid patients exist. In one type, the introspective self is weak and the rigid façade self is held together by strong intellectualization. In another type, the façade self is not weak so much as warped. The patient clings to his or her inappropriate behavioral repertoire and refuses to change it (thereby behaving rigidly), or else escapes into the fantasy of his or her introspective self. Why should the façade self be weak? Perhaps the child's early experience was so traumatic that learning is impaired? Or perhaps the child has neurological damage that impairs learning.

If both the façade self and the introspective self are well developed but in conflict, then symptoms of neurosis will occur. Wagner discussed various kinds of structural possibilities that lead to neurotic symptoms.

1. A simple conflict exists between the façade self and the introspective self.
2. Discrepancies exist between the façade self, the introspective self and the environment. As a result the patient engages in self-deprecatory ruminations (leading to anxiety) or blames others (leading to anger and hostility).
3. In the hysterical personality, the introspective self is underdeveloped, and the patient tries to deal with the environment with a rigid façade self. Alien impulses (particularly sexual and aggressive ones) are prevented from having any behavioral expression. The rigid façade self is weak, immature, and passive, but socially appropriate. The façade self is disconnected from emotional reactivity, that is to say, an event can elicit an emotional response viscerally speaking but is denied awareness and behavioral expression. The façade self does not permit alien impulses (particularly sexual and aggressive impulses) to have any behavioral expression. Insight is poor, because the introspective self is underdeveloped and because the façade self does not permit the expression of certain tendencies or impulses.
4. In the dissociative neuroses, the façade self is similar to that of the hysterical neurotic, but the introspective self is more developed. However, the introspective self is not well integrated with the façade self and so is not readily manifest in the patient's behavior.

    In both the hysteric neurotic and the dissociative neurotic, the façade self is rigid, pseudosocialized, weak, and immature. But it is socially appropriate. The façade self is disconnected from visceral reactivity, so that visceral responses occur, but they are denied awareness and behavioral expression. Wagner emphasizes that a rigid façade self is inimical to the expression of impulses.

    In the hysteric neurotic, stimuli from the environment create a visceral response, but they fail to have a cognitive response due to the impaired introspective self. The inner turmoil is neutralized through the development of physical incapacities. The weakness of the introspective self precludes fantasy outlets and cognitive outlets for the visceral emotional responses. The façade self does not permit behavioral expression of the emotional responses, or rather, does not have a behavioral repertoire that includes action tendencies that are capable of expressing the forbidden wish.

5 Psychopaths (antisocial personality disorder) have a functioning façade self and a weak introspective self. What differentiates them from other character disorders and from the hysteric neurotic is that their façade selves have a veneer of social skills that facilitates the manipulation of others without the investment of any genuine emotion (positive or negative). Psychopaths are not necessarily aggressive, criminal, or sexually disturbed. Since their introspective selves are weak, they have a poor self-concept, are poor at long-range planning, and are deficient in responsibility, fantasy and imagination, and individuality. Their primitive emotional needs, although weak, demand immediate gratification without regard for others, and their façade selves have the behavioral repertoire necessary for such gratification.

It can be seen that Wagner makes use of one other concept other than the strength of the façade and introspective selves, namely that of their content. Is the façade self rigid? Does it possess a behavioral repertoire to permit manipulation or the expression of emotions? Does the introspective self deal cognitively with emotions?

Wagner's views are similar to Angyal's discussion of the neurotic pattern of vicarious living (the hysteric neurotic), and Wagner uses his theory most extensively to describe the hysteric neurotic and the psychopath, both of whom Angyal classified in the pattern of vicarious living. However, Wagner is also able to successfully describe other disorders, and in particular schizophrenic psychoses.

W. B. Yeats: The Anti-Self

Parini (2005) presented the concept of subselves developed by the Irish poet W. B. Yeats. According to Parini, Yeats felt that our masks were anti-selves, and that there was a constant dialectic between the self and the anti-self. In this dialectic, we take on various anti-selves, test them, and then discard them or subsume them into our other selves. For Yeats, the mask was always in place, even with those we love and those with whom we feel most intimately connected.

Is it possible to not wear a mask if the medium for communication is no longer face-to-face? If the interpersonal connection is, for example, only in the written word (for example, by letter or by e-mail), can the mask be cast off? My experience says that this is possible. In the past, I have written to close friends in a "stream of consciousness," without correcting anything I typed – not even one single typing error. (This was easier in the days of typewriters when correcting mistakes was time-consuming.) I have had close friends from whom I held back nothing – to whom I have spoken of things that I would never tell a psychotherapist or someone I loved. But this may never be possible in face-to-face interactions.

Discussion

This section has reviewed the theories of five personality theorists and one poet who have analyzed the concepts of the real self and the façade self. Each uses different terms for this distinction, and each embeds the terms in a theory that has unique connotations and implications. Some of these conceptualizations are more well known than others, and the reader may prefer one over the others. However, Angyal seems on the whole correct in asserting that the pattern of vicarious living has been a common proposal from personality theorists over the years.

COROLLARY 3b: For some people, the façade self may become so pervasive that people come to believe that it is their real self.

This corollary was suggested by Kelly (1965) who used the example of a child wearing a Halloween mask. Kelly asked, "…..is that youngster disguising himself or is he revealing himself?" (p. 158). He continued, "But masks have a way of sticking to our faces when worn too long" (p. 158). Monte and Sollud (2003) noted that some people fall into the mistake that they *are* the role that they portray. This is especially common among professionals such as police officers, psychotherapists and professors. I remember one argument with my wife in which she asked whether I would like to have a blackboard and a piece of chalk![5]

---

[5] Professors often number their points in their arguments. "There are three things you do that really annoy me: (a), (b) and (c)."

FRITZ PERLS: TOPDOG/UNDERDOG

COROLLARY 3c: Other common sets of subselves are the topdog/underdog, introjected subselves and regressive subselves.

Fritz's Perls's notion of the topdog/underdog subselves is a very engaging idea. The topdog subself was described by Perls (1976) as righteous, authoritarian and a bully. The topdog insists that you "should" or "should not." It demands and threatens catastrophe if you do not follow the demands. The underdog (or bottom dog) reacts by being defensive, apologetic, wheedling, and playing a crybaby. These two subselves strive for control of the mind, and the individual is fragmented into the controller and the controlled.

Perls noted that we assume that the topdog is correct, and yet the topdog may make impossible demands, such as those for perfectionism. For some individuals, the impossibility of meeting the demands for perfection forces the underdog to flee into insanity with the result that the individual has a nervous breakdown.

Regressive and Introjected Subselves

Of course, the concepts of topdog and underdog subselves are similar to he psychoanalytic concepts of superego and id (or, as Perls prefers, the superego and the *infraego*), but the superego, id and ego are simply subsets of desires rather than holistic subsystems. Perls's concepts are closer to Eric Berne's Parent and Child ego states.

Some subselves were formed in childhood and adolescence and, as adults, these regressive subselves may assume executive power. This happens in Berne's theory of Transactional analysis when the Child ego-state assumes executive control, either appropriately, when the person is at a party, or inappropriately, when the person is supposed to be an Adult or Parental ego-state.

Subselves may also be introjected, that is, based on the behavior of others. Façade selves clearly form from introjecting the demands made on us by others. However, in the course of development, we may encounter characters in stories, television shows and movies who provide a model for us. Famous individuals or those who become newsworthy may also provide models. One of my living models was Albert Einstein, and one of my fictional anti-models was the character

Oblomov in the novel by Ivan Goncharov of the same name. I resolved never to resemble Oblomov![6]

SOCIAL GROUP MEMBERSHIPS

COROLLARY 3d: Subselves may be defined in terms of social group membership or personal attributes and, in some people, there may be mixed types.

This corollary is based on the ideas of Reid and Deaux (1996) who defined these two types of what they called "identities": (i) collective/allocentric/social versus (ii) individualistic/private/idiocentric/personal. Social identities are based on group memberships, but in the examples given by Reid and Deaux, these are not always roles. Their examples included sex, ethnicity, occupation and religious affiliation. However, some of their examples do approximate roles, such as activist, brother, friend, and student. To the extent that social identities include roles, social identities can be the basis for subselves. In contrast, examples of personal identities given by Reid and Deaux include disciplined, good listener, not gifted, logical, fun and skeptical, merely a set of personality traits.

Trafimow, Triandis and Goto (1991) described two possibilities. In the first, all of the social and personal traits are stored in a single cognitive structure (the one-basket model). In the second, personal attributes are stored in a separate cognitive structure from social attributes (the two-basket model). Reid and Deaux, on the other hand, suggested that the two alternatives were [1] separate identity structures for the personal and the social selves, versus [2] an integrated model with several structures (or clusters) in which each structure (or cluster) contains both social and personal attributes. They gave as an example of such a cluster: brother, friend, good listener, advice-giver and fun.

Reid and Deaux tried to test which of these models was found in their subjects, and concluded that their data was consistent with the segregation model (option [1]). However, Reid and Deaux were not examining subselves, but rather the ways in which self-described traits or attributes cluster. If we switch to a consideration of subselves, it is reasonable to assume that some individuals will label their subselves in social terms ("I am a professor, husband, father, and

---

[6] Oblomov spends most of the novel lying on a sofa thinking about what he might do. Only when he falls in love does he leave the sofa. But, after he has wooed his love and she has agreed to marry him, he returns to his sofa, whereupon his love rejects him.

friend") and others in personal terms ("I have a depressed subself, a happy subself, and occasionally one which has achieved sartori"). When asked to describe the attributes of these subselves, some individuals may choose social attributes, other personal attributes and still others mixed attributes.

The relevant point here is that some subselves may be labeled (and described) in social terms while others may be described in personal terms.

DO SUBSELVES COME IN PAIRS?

COROLLARY 3e: Some subselves may occur in pairs with complementary attributes, whereas other subselves may occur in pairs with similar attributes. It is a clinical question as to whether individuals have such pairs, what is the genesis of these pairs and why some complement each other while others do not.

Boulding (1968), in writing about the subsystems of society, noted that each system tends to create the need for an opposing system that balances it, and that typically these two subsystems share similar characteristics. A forceful pro-choice movement for abortion leads to the development of a forceful pro-life anti-abortion movement, and vice versa. Tough employers and tough unions go together.

This might occur also in subselves. Carl Jung (Progoff, 1973) felt that each complex in the conscious mind was balanced by a complementary complex in the unconscious mind with opposed traits. For example, if the conscious complex is extraverted and prone to use intuition, then the unconscious complex will be introverted and prone to use sensing. Jung saw complexes and subcomplexes balanced in extraversion-introversion, thinking-feeling and sensing-intuition. A similar idea was proposed by Vargiu (1974), with subpersonalities (to use his terminology) developing as a reaction against others.

Freeing this idea from the polarity of conscious/unconscious,[7] it can be proposed that any subself will tend to encourage the development of another subself with complementary characteristics. An example here is the proposal by Perls in his description of Gestalt Therapy, discussed above, of the topdog and underdog.

---

[7] It is possible that there are subselves with only conscious elements or only unconscious elements, but it is more likely that each subself contains both conscious and unconscious elements.

CONCLUSIONS

This chapter has described some common subselves that all (or most of us) may have. The suggestions put forward (real self and façade self; topdog/underdog, and regressive and introjected subselves) are not meant to exhaust the list of possible common subselves. Other proposals may be possible, and I hope that readers will think of some possibilities themselves.

Chapter 4

SUBSELVES AND GROUP DYNAMICS

> If there are times when a Gemini person makes you think you're seeing double, don't run out and change your glasses. Just remember that Gemini is the sign of the twins, and there are two distinct sides to his changeable personality.....He may be one place today and somewhere else tomorrow.....A Gemini can change his clothes, his job, his love life or his residence as fast as he changes his mind, and that's pretty fast.
>
> Goodman (1968, p. 94)

POSTULATE 4: The subselves function in a manner similar to a small group of individuals.

Lester (1985) suggested the usefulness of viewing the various subselves in the mind as a small group. This perspective generates a number of postulates and corollaries.

In group dynamics research, intragroup conflict is typically seen as counterproductive, expending energy on activities unrelated to the group purpose. Shapiro and Elliott (1976) demonstrated the usefulness in psychotherapy of creating new subselves in clients for to reducing this intragroup conflict. For example, it is useful to have a subself with the function of "recording secretary" for information storage, another with the function of "mediator," and sometimes a "chairman of the board" with the power to help resolve conflict between the subselves. In addition, occasional subselves may outlive their use and should be encouraged to "retire" or no longer try to influence the individual's mind.

Lester (1986) noted that small groups with a hierarchical structure are often more productive, but their members are less satisfied. On the other hand, some structure is often useful. The goal is perhaps to have a dominant subself, but not one that is overly dominating.

Research on group dynamics also indicates that egalitarian small groups typically produce more and better solutions to problems than individuals, but that they take longer to reach decision and are more likely to make risky decisions. Perhaps these same principles might apply to people with many subselves. For example, it has been proposed by Andras Angyal (1965), Eric Berne (1961) and Carl Jung (Progoff, 1973) that subselves that are excluded from ever assuming control of the mind exert pressure on the dominant (and domineering) subself, often intruding upon (and even invading) the dominant subself, leading to psychological disturbance.

These ideas can be summarized in a corollary.

COROLLARY 4a: Some subselves collaborate in groups or teams, while others may be isolates; some appear in many situations while others may appear on only rare, special occasions; some are domineering while others are submissive.

Having raised the possibility that subselves can work as a group, creating internal dialogues, it is interesting to bring in some principles from group dynamics and apply them to subselves.

THE PRINCIPLES OF GROUP DYNAMICS APPLIED TO SUBSELVES

Conflict

In Cattell's (1948) group syntality theory, synergy refers to the energy available for a group and is made up of the energy each member brings to the group. Maintenance synergy is used to establish cohesion and harmony in the group. Effective synergy is used to achieve the goals of the group. The more synergy that goes toward maintenance, the less goes toward achieving goals. By analogy, the more psychological effort used to maintain cohesion and harmony between the subselves, the less energy available for achieving the individual's. The more conflict, inconsistency or dissonance (Festinger, 1957), then the less productive the individual will be. Vargiu (1974) has noted that achieving harmony and resolving conflict may also require the various subselves to change, and this requires effort.

On the whole, members of cohesive groups communicate more with one another, are friendlier and more cooperative, have more influence over one another, are more effective in achieving their goals, and are more satisfied (Shaw, 1976, p. 223). By analogy, if the subselves are in conflict with one another, then the person will be less effective in achieving his or her goals and will be more discontented.

Hierarchical Control

Morse and Reimer (1956) compared groups with hierarchical authority structures and groups where the members have more equal amounts of power. They found that the egalitarian groups were more satisfied, but that productivity was greater in the groups with a hierarchical power structure. This suggests that, when the subselves are equal participants in the mind, the individual will be better adjusted. However, when some subselves assume more power in the control of the mind, the person may be more productive. The "workaholic" or driven individual seems to be an appropriate example of this.

These ideas are common themes in group dynamics. Shaw (1976) noted that moderately dominant group members contribute to effective group functioning while extremely dominant members inhibit group functioning. Thus, subselves which become overly dominant may well impede effective functioning of the mind. The problem here, of course, is making decisions based on incomplete information. An extremely dominant subself may act decisively, but may act on incomplete information.

The formation of strong leaders in groups tends to lead to centralized networks of communication. Centralized networks lead to effective problem solving for simple problems, but less efficient problem solving for complex problems. Morale tends to be lower in centralized networks and conformity tends to be less since there is less peer pressure on each member to conform. Thus, it seems plausible that minds with a dominant subself that assumes a leadership role will have more internal conflict since the less dominant subselves will conform less to the final decision.

There is a good illustration of this in Jung's theory. For Jung, when the conscious complexes take over the domination of the mind, the unconscious complexes try to intrude their own perspective, leading to neurosis. For example, a person whose conscious complex uses the thinking function will have the feeling unconscious complexes intrude material into the conscious complexes.

When confronted with difficult tasks, group members are more likely to struggle amongst themselves for the leadership role. This leads to a more contentious group. A similar process smay occur when the mind has to confront a difficult task.

Group Size

Shaw (1976) noted that, as the size of the group increase, the participation of each group member in the group decreases, there is a greater probability that a leader will emerge, the satisfaction of each group member decreases, and conformity to group decisions increases. These ideas suggest that as the number of subselves in the mind increases, the probability increases that a dominant subself will emerge, conformity to final decisions will be more likely, and there will be less satisfaction. What is crucial is that the dominant subself does not become overly dominant and suppress other subselves.

As I noted in Chapter 1, in writing on subselves, Allport (1961), Rowan (1990), and Shapiro and Elliott (1976) have suggested that from 4 to 10 subselves is ideal. Psychotherapists who work with clients using a subself perspective have noted many more subselves in some clients, occasionally claiming that a client had "hundreds" of subselves. A number of subselves this large may be less productive.

Several empirical studies have been reported on this issue. Rowan (1990) asked the clients in a group he led to list their subselves. The mean number listed was 6.5 with a range of zero to eighteen. Lester (1992) asked a sample of undergraduate students to list their subselves and found a mean number of 3.5 with a range of two to six. The number of subselves reported in Lester's study was not associated with age, but the women reported more subselves than the men (with means of 3.8 versus 2.5). The number of subselves reported was also associated with neuroticism and extraversion scores. The extraverted neurotics reported the most subselves, with a mean of 4.6. Lester (2003) found that the number of subselves reported was not associated with cognitive complexity measures from George Kelly's REP Grid (Kelly, 1955), having a Taoist orientation, or scores on Altrocchi's (1999) plural-self scale.

Self monitoring (Snyder, 1987) refers to the tendency of some people to observe and control their self-presentation and expressive behavior. This enables them to communicate their true emotional state by their expressive behaviors and style (such as tone of voice, facial expression, and body posture) and also to communicate an emotional state that is not their true state but which conceals their true state. Lester (1997) gave 96 college undergraduates Snyder's test of self-monitoring and asked them how many subselves they had. The students listed 2.8 subselves on the average with a standard deviation of 2.1. Many of the students did not list any subselves, and their mean self-monitoring score was 10.4, whereas those who listed two or more subselves had a significantly higher self-monitoring score of 12.3. For those listing two or more subselves, the number of subselves listed was not significantly associated with their self-monitoring score. Thus, in this study, those who reported a single self obtained lower self-monitoring scores.

Group Versus Individual Judgments

Shaw also noted that groups produce superior judgments over individual judgments, they produce more varied and better solutions to problems, they often take more time to complete the task, they learn faster and they often make riskier decisions. By analogy, we can propose that people whose minds are made up of several equally strong subselves and not dominated by one subself, will produce better solutions to problems, may produce riskier decisions, and may take longer to make these decisions.

These considerations lead to several corollaries.

COROLLARY 4b: Subselves may form coalitions within the larger group. These coalitions may improve or impair the functioning of the mind.
COROLLARY 4c: In some productive organizations of subselves, one subself acts as a leader, analogous to the conductor of an orchestra, coordinating the contributions of the other subselves.
COROLLARY 4d: Egalitarian groups of subselves typically result in greater satisfaction for the individual.
COROLLARY 4e: The individual's subselves can reorganize themselves in new ways as they develop and as the situation changes.
COROLLARY 4f: Groups of subselves are best limited at least four and to no more than ten.

THE RATIONALITY OF DECISIONS

Moldoveanu and Stevenson (2001) explored the economic decision-making implications of two models of self: the self as a unified system and the self as a fragmented entity. The multiple self was portrayed by Moldoveanu and Stevenson as an "ever-changing, possibly internally conflicting entity" (p. 295) and as possibly a "[s]plit-self – or schizoid….. – recogniz[ing] the internally incoherent nature of selfhood….." (p. 318). Thus, their description of the multiple was biased and quite negative. They referred to the multiple self as a split self and as schizoid and described it as internally incoherent. Their choice of terminology brings in unwarranted connotations of psychiatric disturbance.

They also proposed that each impulse becomes a fully-fledged 'self,' "capable of purposive, narrowly self-interested action, and able to undertake activities that undermine the interests of the other 'selves,' inhabiting the same physical body" (p. 318). It is clear from the perspective of the present book that Moldoveanu and Stevenson have taken a very narrow and specific conception of the multiple self. They confuse a single wish or desire with an organized subself. Nowhere in the present theory has it been proposed that each wish results in a new subself. Furthermore, Moldoveanu and Stevenson assumed without any rationale that all wishes involve self-interest. Angyal's trend toward homonomy, in contrast, asserts that some of our desires can be to unite with and communicate with others and are, therefore, not merely selfish in nature. Finally, Moldoveanu and Stevenson assert that multiple selves will always be in conflict, and that only a unified self can avoid the conflicts between incompatible desires and engage in logical reasoning. In contrast, it has been argued here that multiple selves can function as a harmonious productive group.

The possibility of a multiple self, incoherent and internally conflicting, poses problems for the economic conception of rational humans making decisions based upon the information that they have. For the present theory of personality, it is important to consider whether the point of view of Moldoveanu and Stevenson is valid.

Some of the models of the mind as made up of subselves imply that decision making might be irrational. For example, in Transactional Analysis, if the Child ego state were to be in control of the mind, then decisions would be made by a subself which resembles the mind of the individual as he or she was as a small child. Such a process would run counter to the idea of "economic man" acting on pure rational economic motives and disciplined self-interest. But not all models of the mind as a group of subselves necessarily result in the possibility of irrational decisions.

As we have seen above, group decision making can result in better decisions than individual decision making. For example, juries in the criminal justice system are predicated on the assumption that a number of, often naïve, individuals can reach a mature and rational decision (see Forsyth, 1990, pp. 172-175). We have noted that groups with hierarchical structure are often more productive, and a structure with a dominant subself, but not one which is overly dominating, is best. We have seen that groups of about five typically function better than larger groups. We have also noted above that some psychotherapists who use the concept of the multiple self, such Shapiro and Elliott (1976) discussed above, endeavor to develop new subselves such as "recording secretary" and "mediator." The individual who possesses those subselves may be more likely to achieve greater rationality in decision-making.

The concept of "economic man," which is at the basis of mainstream economic theory, implies a self-interested, rational and temporally stable individual. Although a model which conceptualizes the mind as made up of multiple selves may seem to run counter to this concept, small groups often make better decisions than individuals acting alone, and so a mind that is a multiplicity of selves who function much like a small group may make better decisions than a mind which is a unified self. The result may not be conflict and incoherence. People with multiple selves may, therefore, make more rational and more adaptive decisions in economic affairs than people with a single, unified self, at least in some situations. There are situations, for example, when a company is best led by a dominant and forceful individual, and other situations where a board of directors acting as a group is better. For individuals, the task is to ascertain which decisions are best made by a single unified self and which by a "pantheon of selves" and which types of pantheons are the most effective.

COROLLARY 4g: Multiple selves may lead to more rational decisions than a unified self in some situations.

Performance Versus Satisfaction

There are three possible outputs from groups of individuals and, therefore, subselves (Koslowski & Ilgen, 2006). First, is the performance good, that is, is the decision that results a good decision according to some criteria, and do the accompanying behaviors achieve their goal? Second, does the functioning of the group meet the members' needs, that is, are they satisfied? Third, are the members willing to remain in the group? Applying this to subselves means that the adequacy of the decisions made may or may not be at odds with the satisfaction of the subselves. It is true that dissatisfied subselves cannot "leave" the group – they are, after all, part of the self - but they can cooperate or they can create conflict. One possible outcome is that the satisfaction of subselves (Corollary 4d) may conflict with the adequacy of the decision making (Corollary 4g).

THE PRINCIPLES OF FAMILY DYNAMICS APPLIED TO SUBSELVES

The study of family dynamics may also provide concepts that are applicable to subself theory. For example, Kilmann and Thomas (1975) classified family conflicts using two dimensions: assertiveness and cooperation. High assertiveness and low cooperation results in *competition*; high assertiveness and high cooperation results in *collaboration*; low assertiveness and low cooperation results in *avoiding*; and low assertiveness and high cooperation results in *accommodation*. These types may be useful for describing the conflict and conflict resolution between sets of subselves.

In order to describe married couples, Fitzpatrick (1988) used the dimensions of: (1) conflict avoidance, (2) assertiveness, (3) sharing, (4) ideology, and (5) autonomy.[8] She described several styles for couples based on these dimensions, two of which may be useful for describing sets of subselves. *Independent types* communicate and negotiate while maintaining their autonomy, and conflict is common. *Separate types* avoid conflict by sharing less but have little sense of togetherness and autonomy.

Fitzpatrick and Ritchie (1994) derived a typology of families based on two dimensions of communication patterns: conversation and conformity. High conversation and high conformity result in *consensual families* in which there is great pressure for everyone to agree. High conversation and low conformity result in *pluralistic families* that have open communication and emotional supportiveness with no pressure to agree with one another. Low conversation and high conformity result in *protective families* that avoid conflict and follow conventional rules of behavior. Finally, low conversation and low conformity result in *laissez-faire* families in which the members interact minimally and act independently. These types of families seem suitable for describing sets of subselves.

---

[8] She used other dimensions that seem less useful for describing subselves (ideology and temporal regularity).

We may, then, propose Corollary 4h.

COROLLARY 4h: The interactions between multiple selves may be usefully described using the concepts that have been proposed to describe family dynamics.

AVOIDING THE DANGER OF GROUPTHINK

What about the danger of "Groupthink"? Janis (1972) analyzed major political decisions that turned out to be fiascoes, decisions such as the decision in 1950 to escalate the Korean War by invading North Korea, and described how groups can sometimes come to develop "shared illusions and related norms that interfere with critical thinking and reality testing" (p. 36). What would prevent groups of subselves from making similar bad decisions?

Janis proposed several solutions at the group dynamics level of analysis, and one of his proposals has applicability at the subself level of analysis. Janis suggested that, when a group is making a decision, "at least one member should be assigned the role of devil's advocate" (p. 215). In Chapter 3 above, Corollary 3e proposed that subselves often come in complementary pairs. A top dog is accompanied by an underdog, a happy subself by a depressed subself. It may be, therefore, that groups of subselves often have a "devil's advocate" already in place to raise objections and prevent shared illusions interfering with critical thinking. This leads to the final corollary of this chapter:

COROLLARY 4i: Groupthink can be avoided by assigning at least one subself to the role of devil's advocate.

Chapter 5

SUBSELVES AND PSYCHOLOGICAL DISTURBANCE

> The notion of the "true" self is romantic, and utterly false. There is no such thing.....In reality, there are thousands of selves in every human being. These mingle and shift, mutate, bond, break into part, reassembling countless times in a single day. (Parini, 2005, p. 59)

PROPOSITION 5: There are many forms of psychological disturbance which can arise from the conceptualization of the mind as consisting of many subselves.

The personality theorist who provides the most comprehensive set of ideas which can be utilized in multiple self theory is Andras Angyal. As we have seen above, Andras Angyal (1965) proposed a theory of personality in which the first principle was that the personality is an organized whole and not a mere aggregate of discrete parts. We cannot understand the mind simply by studying its parts. Angyal used the term whole for the concrete organized object and the term system for the organization (or arrangement) of the whole. The system principle is the basis according to which the whole is organized. Every system has one and only one system principle.

The whole can be conceptually divided into parts, subsystems, each of which has a system principle, and subsystems can be conceptually divided into subsubsystems, and so on. Thus, there is a hierarchy, all the way down to the individual elements of the mind, that is, wishes, thoughts, emotions, and behaviors. Maslow (1970) saw this hierarchy as analogous to looking at an object through a microscope and gradually increasing the strength of the magnification.

At the lowest level of magnification, we see the object as a whole. As we increase the level of magnification, we see the several parts that make up the whole. As we increase the level of magnification, we see smaller and smaller parts until, perhaps, we can see the individual molecules or atoms that are the basis for the whole.

Life can be defined as a process of self-expansion, and Angyal called this the trend toward autonomy. Human life consists of a trend toward increasing autonomy. This is a general direction with many expressions: curiosity, the desire to achieve, the wish to dominate, the need to defend one's integrity and maintain one's inviolacy, or the drive to acquire possessions. Angyal saw little point in making an inventory of all of these manifestations of the trend toward autonomy.

Angyal realized that people also seek to be part of a family, a group, a culture, and the universe, even to surrender themselves to this larger unit (a family or a culture) or to become one with God. These desires constitute the trend toward homonomy. Everyone has both trends, though one trend may be more obvious in one person as compared to others. In Angyal's theory, this double trend (toward autonomy and homonomy) constitute the biopositive (healthy) system principle. Either trend can become distorted and take over the personality. But typically both are always present, working side by side. Making love obviously involves sexual satisfaction, a manifestation of the autonomous trend, but it also involves joining together with another, being concerned with them, and communicating with them. This is a manifestation of the homonomous trend.

Each item of behavior functions as part of several systems. Thus, each behavior has, or can have, many functions. Plastic systems are those in which the parts have variable functions. Rigid systems are those in which each part has a fixed function. A process in a rigid system is a localized happening, but a process in a plastic system can have an impact on neighboring parts. In a plastic system, an individual behavior may at one time be part of one system and, at another time, part of another system. This sharing of parts by different wholes is economical. At the physiological level, the processes of urination and sexual activity for males share the some of the same anatomical structures. At the psychological level, consider a kiss. It can indicate friendship, sexual love, familial love, subordination (e.g., kissing the hand of a Pope), a person to be killed (e.g., Judas Iscariot's betrayal of Jesus), or simply respect (e.g., a European gentleman kissing a woman's hand).

As we develop, the parts become differentiated and reorganized. The different parts of the system become increasingly interrelated, and subparts differentiate from the parts that already exist. Integration has to occur to keep the whole intact. In vertical integration, the specific behaviors you manifest must be tied to your particular expressions of the trends toward autonomy and homonomy. Typically the integration moves from the middle toward the depths and the surface. We know what we seem to have chosen to do. I am a professor and a writer. As I develop, I become more skilled in both tasks, that is, my surface behaviors become better suited to achieving my goals. But I also go though crises when I ask myself if this is what I really want to be doing. Do I want to be a professor? Are my day-to-day surface activities related to my deeper trends? Eventually, it would be good if there were a continuity between my deeper trends and my surface behaviors.

Progressive integration refers to the process by which we attain particular goals through particular means. Sometimes people fail to achieve goals, which suggests that they are using inappropriate means. I have a friend who almost has five graduate degrees. He did not pay the final fees necessary to receive his Master's in Education, is one course short of an M.S.W. and two courses short of an M.B.A., has completed 2 of the 3 years of law school, and did everything but the dissertation for a Ph.D. degree. He has a problem in his progressive dimension in this one area of his life!

Since we have several subsystems, and many subsubsystems, and so on, these parallel structures require transverse integration. These parallel structures must be coordinated (unless they are completely independent of one another, a situation that is unlikely except perhaps in disorders such as multiple personality).

Serious problems can occur with transverse integration. Particularly with plastic systems, it is important for the mind to be able to set and shift set easily and appropriately. For example, let us say that two of my subsystems are the role I have at work as a professor and my role at home as a husband. I have to be able to set in each role at the appropriate time. In class, I have to be organized as a professor and stay in that role. I have to set in the role. However, when I arrive home, I have to shift set and switch into my role as husband. If I stay in the role of professor, I may alienate my wife who may resent being treated like a student.

If subsystems are not allowed sufficient time for release, that is, sufficient time in control of the mind, symptoms occur. If one subsystem is much stronger than and dominates the other subsystem, the subordinate subsystem can only inhibit the dominant subsystem rather than share control of the mind. This leads to symptoms of pressure such as tenseness and nervousness.

As the subordinate subsystem gets stronger, it can sometimes interfere with the functioning of the dominant subsystem, leading to symptoms of intrusion such as obsessions, compulsions, and excessive fantasy. As the subordinate subsystem gets even stronger, it can fight the dominant subsystem on equal terms and, if alternative sharing of control of some kind is not possible, then symptoms of invasion, may occur in which the person's behavior is chaotically controlled by two systems at the same time without coordination, leading to symptoms such as indecision, ambivalence, states of confusion, and catastrophic reactions.

Angyal tried to maintain a holistic perspective when he considered disturbed behavior. His terms for healthy and disturbed behavior were biopositive and bionegative, but these adjectives referred to the organization of the mind, not to its contents. For Angyal, the mind is either completely healthy or completely disturbed depending upon the system principle organizing it. If the organizing system principle is a healthy one, then the mind is completely healthy; if the organizing principle is an unhealthy one, then the mind is completely disturbed.

How then can an individual be a "little disturbed"? Angyal saw this as a matter of the relative amount of time for which the healthy and the unhealthy system principles were in control. In the healthy person, the healthy system principle organizes the mind for most of the time; in the disturbed person, the unhealthy system principle organizes the mind for most of the time.

Maslow (1942) conducted a study of the sexual behavior of healthy and unhealthy women. He devised a psychological test to measure their psychological health and questioned them about their sexual history. He found that the psychologically healthy women were more likely to have engaged in all kinds of sexual behavior, including those that some in our society might consider perverted. Maslow reflected on this and concluded that there was not such a thing as a "perverted" behavior. There were, however, "perverted" people. However healthy people behaved, whatever they did was healthy because their minds were organized by a healthy system principle. In contrast, whatever a disturbed person did is unpleasant. The way in which such a person looks at you, shakes your hand, or eats food is unpleasant!

His students once asked Maslow whether a psychologically healthy person could murder another. "Of course," he replied. It is the organization of the mind that determined the "goodness" or "badness" of the act. Killing for the correct reasons can be the act of a healthy person. Had one of Adolf Hitler's potential assassins succeeded in killing him, that person would have saved millions from death and been viewed as a hero of the 20th Century.

Unhealthiness is, then, a way of life for Angyal. It is an organization with its own goals, attitudes, and motivations, and may lead to symptoms of pressure, intrusion, and invasion as it competes with the healthy way of life. Personality (or our mind) is, therefore, by necessity, a dual organization, each of the organizations governed by a different system principle -- the principle of universal ambiguity.

Whereas Angyal proposed two system principles, biopositive and bionegative, in multiple self theory we can consider them to be two subselves which vie for control of the mind. Each subself defends itself against the rival system; the defense mechanisms are the tactics used by each system. The traditional psychoanalytic defense mechanisms (such as sublimation and projection) are ways in which the unhealthy system tries to prevent the healthy system from taking over control of the mind. Angyal noted that psychologists needed to define a set of defense mechanisms that the healthy system uses to prevent the unhealthy system from taking over. He suggested processes that he called empathy, objectivity, and inventive thought, terms that do not appeal to me. A better set of defense mechanisms for the healthy system comes from the strategies proposed by systems of psychotherapy, such as disputing irrational beliefs (which is used in cognitive therapy), uncovering the unconscious contributions to our behavior (which is used in psychoanalysis), and becoming more aware of our emotions (which is used in Gestalt therapy).

Angyal proposed two patterns for the neurotic system principle (see Chapter 3). The method of adjustment in the *pattern of vicarious living* is the systematic repression of one's genuine personality and an attempt to replace it with a substitute personality. This substitute personality has been called the social self, the pseudo-self and the façade self - the self we present to others and by means of which we seek to hide our real self.

The *pattern of noncommitment* results in a person who is confused as to whether the world is basically good and friendly versus bad and hostile. This leads to uncertainty and ambivalence. These people express fear and hostility toward a presumably hostile world, seem confused and indecisive, and adopt techniques to dispel the confusion such as obsessions, compulsions, and rituals.

There are two other holistic theories of personality that have concepts that are useful for understanding psychological disturbance in multiple self theory: Eric Berne's Transactional Analysis and Carl Jung's Analytic Psychology.

TRANSACTIONAL ANALYSIS

Berne (1961, 1964) proposed three new theories: a theory of personality, a theory of interpersonal relationships, and a system of psychotherapy. This section only discusses his theory of personality, which he has called structural analysis (see Chapters 1 and 3).

Structural analysis is concerned with analysis of ego states, and the concept of ego states is similar to the concept of subselves. People are always in some ego state. They can shift from one to another, and these ego states are usually Parent, Adult, or Child ego states. When people shift from one ego state being predominant to another being predominant, Berne talks of psychic energy flowing from one state to another, a concept in the theory that is unnecessary for modern theories of the mind. The state that is predominant is said to be cathected. (Note that the terms cathect and cathexis are used differently in Berne's theory than in Freud's theory, see Lester [1995]) It has executive power for the moment and is experienced as the real self. Berne also talks of cathexis flowing from one state to another, again in a similar manner as psychoanalytic theory. The use of the terms energy and cathexis seems old-fashioned today. Angyal's terms set and shifting set describe the processes involved in a more modern way and fit better with current psychological theory.

Each ego state is an entity in Berne's theory, which is differentiated from the rest of the psychic contents. It has a boundary that separates it from other ego states. However, the ego boundaries are semipermeable under most conditions. The shift from one ego state to another depends on the forces acting on each ego state, the permeability of the boundaries of each ego state, and the capacity of each ego state to be cathected.

Ego states can affect behavior directly by being the predominant ego state of the moment, or by influencing other ego states (which parallels Angyal's concept of symptoms of pressure). The primary ego state that Berne talks of as having an influence is the Parent. For example, the Child can function as an independent state (free) or under the Parent's influence (adapted).

The basic conceptual units that Berne defined gave him a reasonably large armamentarium with which to describe various psychological disorders. The following sections will look at three types of psychopathology using Berne's structural analysis.

Structural Pathology

Structural pathology is conceptualized in terms of deformities in the structure of the total personality. One ego state may govern exclusively. For example, if the Child ego state governs exclusively, excluding the Adult and Parent ego states completely, we may have a narcissistic impulsive personality (for example, that which a high-class prostitute might have) or an active schizophrenic. The Adult and Parent ego states are said, in this case, to be decommissioned. The Child ego state is experienced as the real self.

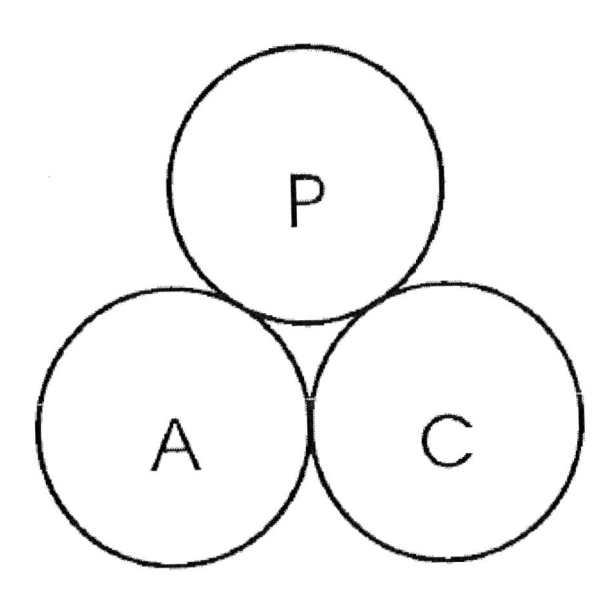

Figure 5.1. An alternative way of depicting the three ego states

A second structural problem is contamination. One ego state intrudes through the other ego state's boundaries. For example, if the Adult ego state contaminates the Child ego state, delusions and hallucinations may occur. In the schizophrenic, the predominant ego state is that of the Child, and the hallucinations and delusions are intrusions from the Parent and Adult ego states, respectively. The Child ego state does not realize that it has been intruded upon because the boundaries are not firm enough to recognize the intrusion for what it is, i.e., that it comes from a source outside the Child ego state boundaries. (Actually Berne says that Child-Parent contamination is not possible, but he also says that hallucinations have their source in the Parent ego state. This is a contradiction.) However, it would seem that Berne intentionally draws the Parent, Adult, and Child ego states on top of each other to emphasize that contamination is only possible, as he sees it, between Parent and Adult and between Child and Adult. Figure 5.1 shows an improved way of drawing the three ego states. Contamination of each ego state by any other is possible in the theory depicted in Figure 5.1. Contamination of the Adult ego state with the Parent ego state, according to Berne, leads to prejudice.

Processes originating from the predominant ego state plus its contaminated areas are ego-syntonic, whereas processes originating from outside the boundary are ego-dystonic. (It is critical, therefore, to investigate whether hallucinations are ego-syntonic or ego-dystonic. Both types of hallucinations are probably possible.) In Berne's conceptualization, the Adult ego state can be contaminated both by the Child and by the Parent ego states.

Some additional illustrations may increase our understanding of how Berne applies his concepts to explaining pathology.

1. Mania results from structural pathology. In mild levels of mania (hypomania), the Child and the Adult ego states exclude the Parent ego state, and the Child dominates (or contaminates) the Adult. However, the Adult still has some influence. In mania proper, the Child excludes the Adult as well. However, the Parent ego state is still monitoring the person's behaviors, and the Child ego state knows it is being watched. Thus, the Child ego state may have delusions of reference and persecution (for example, that people are recording what is taking place). When the Child becomes exhausted, the Parent ego state assumes control and takes revenge, leading to severe depression.

2. Lesions in the boundary between two ego states lead to boundary symptoms, again a form of structural pathology. Lesions of the Child-Adult boundary lead to such symptoms as feelings of unreality, estrangement, depersonalization, jamais vu, and déjà vu.

3. Contamination is important in understanding the difference between dissociated thoughts and delusions. If a thought from the Child ego state becomes conscious to the Adult ego state, the Adult ego state experiences it as a strange idea, a dissociated thought. If however, a contamination has occurred and the Child thought comes from the contaminated area, then the thought is ego-syntonic and may be labeled (by others) as a delusion. The Adult ego state does not realize that it is a thought from outside of its boundary.

4. A person's ego states may be well defined with impermeable boundaries so that he is well organized. However, there may be severe internal conflicts in the ego states. For example, an alcoholic who can segregate

his ego states well may be able to work effectively on his job despite heavy drinking at home.

This example raises an issue that Berne does not address clearly. Can there be several ego states that are Adult, or Child, or Parent? Berne describes contamination and other forms of structural pathology as occurring between two ego states. But, of course, there may be several ego states of each type (Parent, Adult and Child). For example, if the working alcoholic is one ego state and the drunk alcoholic is another, can these two states both be Adult or both be Child, or is one an Adult ego state and the other a Child? Berne is by no means clear on this issue.

5   In psychopathy, and paranoia the Adult ego state is contaminated by the Child ego state (and cooperates with it), but it is not decommissioned. This is similar to the state of affairs in hypomania and mild depression.

6   In neurosis, the Adult ego state is contaminated by the Child and Parent ego states, and the Parent ego state is the prime enemy. During free association, the Child ego state can talk while the Adult and Parent ego states listen. The censorship of the Parent ego state is suspended. (In contrast, during hypnosis and narcoanalysis the Adult and Parent ego states are temporarily decommissioned.)

Functional Pathology

Psychological disorder is also described in terms involving the lability of cathexis (that is, the ease or difficulty in shifting from one ego state to another), and the permeability of ego state boundaries. For example, a person may show a stubborn resistance to shifting ego states, or may shift opportunistically. Ego state boundaries can be firm or soft, and the softer they are the easier contamination is. Cathexis may be viscous, which would make shifting ego states difficult. (What this process is supposed to mean other than that shifting set is difficult is hard to imagine. It would have been easier to understand if Berne had simply said that some people are sluggish in shifting ego states.)

Content Pathology

Berne does not label a third source of pathology, but he implies one. He says that Parent, Adult, and Child ego states can all be syntonic with one another, with no contamination or functional pathology, yet there may be pathology. He gives the example of a happy concentration camp guard. We would see such a person as pathological, not because of any structural or functional pathology in his system of ego states, but because we object to the behaviors, desires, thoughts, and emotions he has. This example, suggests that the content of the ego states may be sufficient to cause pathology..

ANALYTIC PSYCHOLOGY[2]

Analytic psychology is the name by which Carl Jung's theory of personality and psychotherapy is known. Jung's term for the totality of psychological processes was the psyche. Jung proposed that complexes exist within the psyche, autonomous partial systems that are organizations of psychic contents. Complexes are subsystems of the whole. (The complexes in the collective unconscious are identical to the archetypes.) In particular, Jung identified several complexes that he felt were of particular use for a discussion of human behavior.

The ego consists of our conscious psychic contents and contains percepts, memories, thoughts, desires, and feelings. The persona is a subsystem within the ego and is the self that we present to others, the mask we wear in daily intercourse with others. It consists of the roles we play in our lives. Because we have several roles, it makes more sense to speak of various components of the persona.

The shadow consists of those psychic contents in the personal (and to a lesser extent the collective) unconscious that are in opposition to the contents of the ego. These contents are less developed and less differentiated than the contents of the ego, but their presence is made apparent to the ego whenever the boundaries between the systems break down and contents from the shadow intrude into the ego.

In addition, the subsystem in the collective unconscious that is in opposition to the persona subsystem of the ego is called the anima in males and the animus in females. By modern standards, Jung erred here in identifying the core of human behavior in terms of the social sexual stereotypes of his day. Jung described males as "masculine" and females as "feminine," in what today would be considered a gender-biased fashion. For example, Jung described the unconscious animus of females as rational and discriminating, showing that Jung believed females to have inevitably an irrational and emotional conscious ego. Today, we have no need to accept all of Jung's ideas wholesale. We can better conceptualize the anima and animus as the subsystems of the shadow that are in opposition to the

---
[9] This discussion of analytic psychology is based on Progoff (1973).

persona and that permit their content to vary depending upon the psychic contents of the particular persona. (Perhaps we could call these both "animum," using the Latin neuter gender?)

The self is the part of the psyche that eventually becomes the synthesized whole. The self represents the combination of the opposed parts of the psyche organized into a unified whole.

Psychic Functions and Attitudes

Jung suggested that the psyche responds to stimuli (internally or externally generated) by sensing them, interpreting them, evaluating them, and sometimes having an immediate awareness of them. He called these functions sensation, intuition, thinking, and feeling. He suggested that these functions are developed to differing degrees within each person, thereby providing a basis for categorizing people. Jung conceptualized these functions in pairs: sensing versus intuition, thinking versus feeling. The ego typically develops one of these functions more fully than others, and the opposite function of the pair becomes the strongest function of the shadow.

Jung also distinguished two attitudes of the psyche. The attitude of extroversion orients the person toward external stimuli; the attitude of introversion orients the person toward internal stimuli. If the conscious part of the psyche (the ego) adopts one attitude, then the personal unconscious (the shadow) will have the other attitude.

Abnormal Behavior

Abnormal behavior can result from various causes in the psyche. The goal of the psyche is to unite into a complete whole, a process called individuation. Perhaps in order to unite, the psyche has to fragment into various subsystems first. Abnormal behavior can result from one subsystem becoming dominant over another or from one subsystem taking over the system of which it is but a part. For example, in some people the persona takes over the ego. The person who was presenting himself as a teacher initially now becomes a Teacher. Other aspects of his ego are suppressed by the persona.

Neurosis for Jung was a term to describe the condition in which a group of psychic contents (a complex) moves from the unconscious and disturbs the conscious. It occurs whenever any particular system or subsystem (or complex) has become overdifferentiated from the others. The goal of the unconscious is to restore the balance in the psyche whenever the conscious psychic contents begin to dominate the psyche. The more the conscious systems become autonomous, the more the unconscious systems will become autonomous, leading to an inner cleavage in the psyche. Thus, a neurosis is a state of being at war with oneself, a dissociation of personality. To cure a neurosis, the contending systems (and their system principles) must be fused into a new entity, greater than either alone (that will then be the "self"). The integration of the psyche, therefore, requires that it first split.

If a person grows up in a society that contains conflicting values and ideas, this dissociation of the psyche is facilitated. If, on the other hand, a person identifies with an established belief system in the society, then neurosis is less likely.

A psychosis is differentiated from a neurosis only by the degree of control exerted by the conscious part of the psyche over the unconscious complexes. In a psychotic person, elements of the unconscious intrude into the conscious ego. If the intrusion is partial, the ego may merely continue to exist with this unassimilated element. If the intrusive element is integrated into the ego, the ego may identify with it and accept it as an ego-derived element. Perhaps a psychotic who hears a voice has an unassimilated element deriving from the unconscious; one who has a delusion has identified with an autonomous (partial) complex from the unconscious. In a neurotic, the conscious elements of the ego remain in control of the psyche; in a psychotic, the unconscious elements are in control.

The neurotic will have symptoms that stress their weakest activity. For example, if the ego has most fully developed the thinking function, the neurotic will have symptoms involving feeling activities. The symptom, therefore ,describes what the ego is not doing; it establishes an agenda and points to the direction that the psyche must take.

The infant's psyche is undifferentiated and whole. Maturation and growth lead to differentiation and splitting of psychic contents. Psychological health involves synthesis of the separate parts. The basic goal of the psyche then is integration, or individuation. Individuation involves the balancing and harmonizing of the psyche. Jung's concepts typically involve opposed systems, processes, functions, and attitudes, and so synthesis of these opposites makes an obvious end state for the psyche to attain. This feature of Jung's ideas is sometimes called "the principle of opposites." The majority of the "splits" in the psyche that Jung considered involve splits between conscious elements or complexes and unconscious elements or complexes. The splits could, of course, be between conscious elements or, alternatively, between unconscious elements, but such splits were not considered as important.

The proposals made by Angyal, Berne and Jung lead to the following corollaries.

COROLLARY 5a: The system principle of a subself may be pathological.

This comes from Angyal's proposal of the patterns of vicarious living and noncommitment which constitute his bionegative system principle.

COROLLARY 5b: Psychological disturbance can arise from symptoms of pressure, intrusion, and invasion between subselves.

As we have seen above, this description of psychological disturbance was proposed most cogently by Angyal. In symptoms of pressure, one subself tries to assume executive power while another subself is in control. This can result in mild symptoms such as insomnia, heightened anxiety, restlessness and fatigue.

In symptoms of invasion (called *contamination* by Berne), while one subself has executive power, other subselves affect occasional behaviors. The tone of voice or other nonverbal qualities of the behavior may be controlled by a suspended subself. Slips of the tongue, obsessive thoughts, hallucinations and delusions are other manifestations of symptoms of intrusion. Jung considered neurosis to be the result of intrusions.

In symptoms of invasion, subselves invade one another, and the behavior of the individual becomes chaotic as different behaviors are controlled by different subselves. It is a state of being at war with oneself, and Jung saw the psychoses as the manifestation of symptoms of invasion.

COROLLARY 5c: Psychological disturbance can arise when one subself has executive power exclusively.

When one subself governs exclusively, the other subselves are deprived permanently of executive power, and this creates an imbalance amongst the subselves. The ideal situations is for each subself to be recognized, accepted and permitted expression and to have executive power from time to time. Berne saw each of the three ego states that he proposed (Child, Adult and Parent) as being appropriate in some situations and, therefore, each ego state should assume executive power from time to time. The same proposal can be made for subselves.

Related to this, we may propose the following corollary which comes from the discussion of multiple selves based on the principles of group dynamics in Chapter 4.

COROLLARY 5d: It can be healthy for one subself to maintain overall control of the group of subselves while allowing each subself to have executive power from time to time or delegating duties to other subselves. It may be pathological when this "chairman of the board" is impaired in its role, for this may lead to conflict, struggles and even war between the subselves, rendering the person's mind chaotic.

Conflict between subselves can be avoided by having good communication between them, validating the existence and function of each subself, and by strengthening the "chairman of the board."

COROLLARY 5e: Psychological disturbance can arise when the individual has difficulty setting and shifting set (changing which subself has executive power) appropriately in a situation.

Difficulties in setting and shifting set were discussed by both Angyal and Berne. A person may show a stubborn resistance to shifting subselves when a shift is warranted, as when the role that the individual is operating needs to change (from worker to parent, for example), or when the individual shifts sets opportunistically and inappropriately (for example, when a psychotherapist commits a boundary violation and becomes sexually intimate with a client).

COROLLARY 5f: Psychological disturbance can arise when the content of the subselves is pathological.

There may be psychopathology because the content of one or more subselves is pathological. A serial murderer may, for example, have several subselves with firm boundaries (and so no symptoms of intrusion or invasion) and be able to set and shift set appropriately, and yet may enjoy torturing and killing others

COROLLARY 5g: The healthiest individuals may have one subself that is in charge of the set of subselves.

Frick (1993) suggests that a superordinate subself, is required for healthy functioning or, as some have phrased it (e.g., Schwartz, 1995), someone to conduct the orchestra.

> Ultimately, important life decisions and commitments must be made – a commitment to one set of needs rather than another, to one value system among competing values, and to one set of potentials rather than another. Although these commitments and values may change over time, it seems to me that one integrated and central self-system – one superordinate voice – is always required to sort through these issues in one's life and to make choices (Frick, 1993, p. 127)

There may also be a core subself than can and should assume leadership.

This principle is similar to one found in group dynamics. In the classic study by Kurt Lewin and his colleagues (Lewin, et al., 1939), groups of 10 and 11 year-old boys were led by an adult who took one of three styles: autocratic (who made all the decisions for the group), democratic who let the group make the decisions under his guidance and with his advice) and laissez-faire (who let the boys function by themselves, rarely offering information, criticism or guidance spontaneously). The laissez-faire groups spent much less time working on the projects than the other two sets of groups. However, the autocratic groups worked less when when the leader was absent, were more discontented, made more demands for attention and were showed less friendliness. Overall, groups with a democratic leader functioned best.

> COROLLARY 5h: Some subselves may cease to be useful as the individual matures and may need to become less influential in determining the individual's life.

Hermans (2002) discussed the case of "Nancy," a client he treated, who decided that she no longer wanted a subself she named the "child" to determine her life. Nancy was 47 years old, had two adolescent children and worked as a secretary. Her presenting symptoms were mainly psychosomatic and included headaches and muscular tension. She felt that she always had to defend her place in the world and was overly dependent on the approval of others which led her to being a perfectionist.

Nancy was given a list of "positions" from which she chose: fighter, vulnerable figure, self-surrender figure, recognition seeker, critic, and child, among others. She was asked to keep a diary in which she recorded the people with whom she was interacting and in which situations and which position she was in at the time. From the diary, it became clear that the child position played a central role in her daily life. Nancy was then asked to take her child position and make valuations from this position and contrast these valuations with ones made from an independent position. For example, "I want attention and I want recognition" was contrasted with "Yes, then you should do it in a good way; not by nagging but by staying realistic; I determine what happens, often in consultation" (p. 89).

Nancy remembered: "As a teenager, my father did not allow me to do much; he was strict and hot-tempered; I was never allowed to say what I thought; he didn't allow me to have any contact with him; I never noticed that he liked me" was contrasted with "I can relativize this [no contact] from the position of independence; he's been dead for a long time; I see better now what happened; I think he was a coward 'cause he clearly chose for my mother; he thought he had to, that he had no choice" (p. 89).

In this way, she worked with her therapist to develop another subself she named the "independent" figure which she introduced into her group of subselves so as to minimize the impact of the "child" subself on her behavior.[10]

> COROLLARY 5i: Subselves that may be unhelpful for some tasks and impair performance and development may be useful in other situations.

Excellent examples of this can be found in Eric Berne's ego states in which each ego state (Child, Adult and Parent) is appropriate in some situations and would be inappropriate in other situations. A colleague of mine who was going through a divorce began breaking down in class, crying and talking about the crisis in his life. From a Transactional Analysis point of view, his Child ego state was taking over in a situation where his Parent ego-state should have been in control. The result was that he was not granted tenure.

> COROLLARY 5j: The possibility of attributing negatively-valued aspects (thoughts, desires, emotions or behaviors) of oneself to one or more subselves may enable the individual to maintain high self-esteem since the negative aspects of one subself do not color the other subselves.

In a discussion of types of self-representations, Markus and Wurf (1987) noted that negative identities and negative self-views can be elaborated into self-schemas. These negative self-schemas can co-exist with overall feelings of high

---

[10] Hermans uses the term "position," but his ideas fit nicely into the present theory of multiple selves.

self-esteem, and they suggested that this is possible if the negative self-schemas are bounded and relatively isolated from the rest of the personality. In the present theory, one or more subselves, therefore, could have a pathological (or less than healthy) content or have a pathological organization, without having a major impact on the other subselves which may be healthy (or biopositive). The extreme case of this is found in cases of multiple personalities where the pathological subself is dissociated and the other subselves have no knowledge of this pathological subself.

CONCLUSION

The present chapter has explored several ways in which a multiple self theory of personality can deal with psychological disturbance (abnormal behavior or bionegativity). Drawing on the theories of Andras Angyal, Eric Berne, Carl Jung and others, psychological disturbance was seen as arising from

- a pathological system principle for a subself
- symptoms of pressure, intrusion and invasion between subselves.
- one subself having executive power exclusively
- difficulties in setting and shifting set
- the content of the subself is pathological
- not having one subself that can take charge
- having subselves that have outlived their usefulness
- having subselves that impair the performance of certain tasks
- not being able to encapsulate negative self-representations into one single subself

In the next chapter, we move on to a discussion of how multiple self theory may guide psychotherapy.

Chapter 6

SUBSELVES AND PSYCHOTHERAPY

De tantos hombres que soy, que somos
No puedo encontrar a ninguno;
Se me pierden bajo la ropa,
Se fueron a otra cuidad.

Of the many men who I am, whom we are
I cannot settle on a single one.
They are lost to me under the cover of clothing
They have departed for another city.

(Pablo Neruda, 1970, pp. 362-363)

Subselves may play a useful role in psychotherapy. For example, Bogart (1994) argued that subselves (which he called personas) can be active players in our efforts to be fully functioning or self-actualized. Bogart used personas in his system of psychotherapy and explored them using Fritz Perls's hot seat technique (Perls, et al., 1951), Virginia Satir's (1967) conjoint family therapy, and Jacob Moreno's psychodrama (Yablonsky, 1976). He had clients write autobiographies for each subself and name them, a process which continues and becomes more precise as the community of selves interact with one another (which he called "multiloguing"). He endeavored to get the subselves and the whole self to grow together toward greater levels of maturity, to shift from one of them wielding power to all of them sharing power. This leads us to Postulate 6.

POSTULATE 6: The concept of subselves is useful for psychotherapy and counseling.

The hypothetical existence of subselves has a long history or use in psychotherapy. As noted in Chapter 5, Transactional Analysis (Berne, 1961) is based on the existence of ego-states. Transactional Analysis begins with a structural analysis in which the clients are introduced to the concept of ego states and helped to identify which ego state is in control at any time. Intrusions of one ego state into another (called contamination in Transactional Analysis) are identified and eliminated. Psychotherapy then moves to a transactional analysis, in which transactions are examined for such issues as whether they are complementary or crossed and overt or covert (as in "games"). Goulding and Goulding (1979) have proposed their own system which also uses ego states, called Redecision Therapy. Carl Jung's Analytic Psychology (see Chapter 5), also uses subselves (called complexes by Jung) as the basis for understanding the mind.

For example, in a case reported by Goulding and Goulding (1978) of a psychiatrist who had made several suicide attempts, they asked him in one session to split his self into two parts. In one chair he played the subself that has not allowed him to kill himself in the past - the part of him (subself) that did not take quite enough pills, that allowed him to be found, and that survived after his heart stopped beating. In the other chair he put the other subself - the one that wanted to die. He then created a dialogue between the two parts of himself.

> I will not let you kill me. I want to be alive and stay alive. I will not let you kill me.
>
> I hear you; you really want to live, don't you. I won't kill you. I won't kill myself.
>
> I am the most powerful part of me and I will not let anything happen to me that ends in my death (Goulding & Goulding, 1978, pp. 181-182)

In the next three sections, we will examine briefly three systems of psychotherapy that utilize concepts similar to those in the multiple self theory of the mind.

TRANSACTIONAL ANALYSIS

In the previous chapter, the relevance of Transactional Analysis for describing and understanding psychological disturbance was discussed. How does Transactional Analysis work with ego states (subselves) in psychotherapy? In the first stage in Transactional Analysis, the psychotherapist meets with the client one-on-one and introduces the client to the concepts of Transactional Analysis, including ego states and contamination. This is called a structural analysis. After this, the client is moved into a group, and the interaction of the group members in their different ego states is explored, a transactional analysis. Transactions can be simple or crossed, overt and covert, and the games in which clients engage (with these overt and covert transactions) are identified. Finally, the client may undergo a script analysis, analyzing their life plan which is conceptualized as if it were a script for a role in a play.

Berne (1961) presented the case of Mrs. Enatosky who came for 15 sessions. She was a 34 year-old housewife with a history of depression who had been an alcoholic but was now "dry" with the help of AA. Initially, she was introduced to the concept of ego states in a structural analysis. In the 2nd session, she talked about wanting approval and rebelling "like a little girl." She was encouraged to let the little girl out. She talked of "parental" expectations for her, and this included both her father and her husband. She was seductive with her husband and behaved similarly with her father. Her parents separated when she was seven, but she said of her father, "I could have kept him."

In the 3rd session she mentioned a feeling of "walking high," and it was pointed out to her that this was her Child ego state. She remembered her mother walking quickly with her and dragging her by the arm. She also recognized the role of her Parent ego state when she disapproved of her son's behavior. In the 4th session, she was shown how her Child, Adult and Parent ego states all operated in her dealings with her son – seductiveness, gratification when he did his work, and disapproval of his behavior, respectively.

The therapist then placed her in a group for the 5th session in order to engage her in a transactional analysis, and he helped her to explore her past in order to discover more about her Child ego state. She saw a connection between her mother telling her to clean up "messes" and the role of AA and the church in cleaning up her psychological messes. For this reason, she gave up both AA and the church. When she asked the psychotherapist whether it was all right to be aggressive, she was encouraged to let her Adult ego state make the decision rather than asking for parental permission (from the therapist).

It became apparent to the therapist that her Child ego state had doubts about its existence. When her mother was eight months pregnant, her husband had tried to poison her. They saved the client, but thought that the mother was going to die. (She survived but was now in a psychiatric hospital.) Mrs. Enatosky often wondered, "Why do I exist? Sometimes I doubted my existence." The therapist suggested that she get a copy of her birth certificate on the assumption that, if her

Adult ego state obtained and saw the birth certificate, it might confirm to her Child ego state that she really did exist.

In the group, the games that she played were discussed. For example, she often "conned" others into parental roles so that she could be in her Child ego state, but she then complained about them for being in control. With her husband, they played "alcoholic," and they alternated the roles of the drinker and the sober partner.

Berne's description of the case is, of course, more detailed than this, but it is clear how the concept of ego states can be useful in helping clients understand their behavior.

REDECISION THERAPY

Goulding and Goulding (1979) are transactional analysts, but they have focused on a different aspect of the system. Injunctions are messages from the Child ego state of parents given to their children at a young age. Goulding and Goulding listed several, such as: *Don't get close, Don't succeed, Don't be smart,* and *Don't exist.* Children have the option of accepting or rejecting these injunctions but, being powerless, they typically accept them. Children may also fantasize, invent and misinterpret what the parents say and, thereby, accept inunctions that were never actually given to them by their parents.

When grown up, individuals may become conscious of what injunctions they were given and accepted, and their Adult ego state may make the redecision to change. But Goulding and Goulding noted that the injunction was accepted by the individual's Child ego state and, therefore, the redecision to change must be made by the Child ego state. If the redecision is made only by the Adult ego state, the individual will develop psychosomatic symptoms or dysfunctional behaviors. For example, an individual may have accepted the injunction to "Work hard." As an adult, his Adult ego state may decide to cut back on his working hours and take more time off, but then he may devote so much effort and time to his hobby (such as golf or fishing) that his "play" becomes "work." In their therapy sessions, for example, the client is encouraged to go back to early scenes, to be a child and to confront their parents – to have their Child ego states make the redecision.

[Therapist]: Are you willing to be a little girl?.....See your Dad and Mom in front of you.....And let yourself be little...And would you see your parents and describe them *(She does)* Would you let yourself see the kind of connection of pain that runs between the two of them?.....And as a little girl would you tell them that you are separate from their pain?

Arda: My mother wouldn't let me separate! *(Sobbing)* I go off in a corner and read and she won't let me. *(She sounds very little.)*

[Therapist]: Well you are separate.....As you go off in the corner, Arda, let yourself know how much you wanted to separate.

Arda: Oh, yes. I couldn't stand the noise and the fighting and the dishes crashing around the walls. I'm so scared, I just wanted to get away, but...no place to go. My mother made me wash my father when he was drunk. I wanted to get away...

[Therapist]: Of course you wanted to get away.....And you deserved to have someone there taking care of you....And letting you know that you are a separate human being.

Arda: I am separate. I can look like you. I can feel good things in you, but I am not you. I don't have to take on your pain. (Goulding & Goulding, 1979, pp 193-194)

VOICE THERAPY

Voice therapy was devised by Robert Firestone (1988) and has three major premises (L. Firestone, 2005).

1. There is within each of us a split between a good self, a life-affirming, goal-directed self, and an "inner demon," a self-critical and self-destructive self. Lisa Firestone (2005) illustrated this with a quote from Sylvia Plath:

   I have a good self, that loves skies, hills, ideas, tasty meals, bright colors. My demon would murder this self by demanding that it be a paragon, and saying it should run away if it is anything less. (Hughes & McCullough, 1982, pp. 176-177)

2. Each of us an inner voice that expresses in words the thoughts and desires of this inner demon, thoughts that range from mild self-criticism to extreme self-hatred.
3. This inner voice leads each of us to engage in self-destructive behaviors. Voice therapy endeavors to give vocal speech to this inner voice so that it can be heard and discussed in therapy. Firestone gave an example of a

therapy session with a female client who, after shouting out this inner voice, said:

> That was so weird, like suddenly someone else was talking through my mouth. Sometimes I think things like that, but this felt like someone else was yelling them at me. And the thing is, that's how it feels, like there's someone in my head telling me these things. Not to be a fool, not to trust anyone, that I need to stand up for myself or I'm just a stupid jerk, that I am a stupid jerk. (Firestone, 2005, p. 269)

This is similar to the automatic thoughts described by Aaron Beck (1976). Beck described the properties of these thoughts as follows:

1. They [automatic thoughts] generally are not vague and unformulated, but are specific and *discrete*. They occur in a kind of shorthand; that is, only the essential words in a sentence seem to occur – as in a telegraphic style.
2. The thoughts do not arise as a result of deliberation, reasoning, or reflection about an event or topic. There is no logical sequence of steps as in a goal-oriented thinking or problem-solving. The thoughts 'just happen.' They just seem to be relatively *autonomous* in that the patient made no effort to initiate them and in more disturbed cases they are difficult to 'turn off.'
3. The patient tends to regard these automatic thought as *plausible* or reasonable, although they may seem far-fetched to somebody else.....The content of automatic thoughts, particularly those that are repetitive and seem to be most powerful, are *idiosyncratic*. (Beck, 1976, pp. 36-37)

There is much overlap between Firestone's concept of the voice and Beck's automatic thoughts.[11]

Firestone (2004) discussed how voice therapy could have helped a young woman who committed suicide at the age of 21, leaving a diary covering the final year of her life. Katie had been sexually abused by her alcoholic father. After he left the home, her mother became psychotic, and Katie and her younger sister were placed separately in a series of foster homes. Katie developed an eating disorder which had required hospitalization on several occasions. At college, Katie had a boy-friend, but her relationship with him raised many problems for

---

[11] Sandbek (1993) proposed a weaker version of voice therapy in his book on the treatment of anorexia and bulimia.

her. In a hypothetical therapy session, Firestone helped Katie explore her inner voice and to shout the words out loud.

> Therapist: It sounds like you have a lot of negative thoughts about yourself. Try saying that again. "I'm a pig and a weak person and I don't deserve anything good" – only this time, say it as if another person was saying it to you about you.
> .....
> Katie: *(Louder voice)* "What is wrong with you? You can't even stick to a diet for one week. You should starve yourself! Eat nothing, you don't deserve anything. You're a loser! Not worth ANYTHING! *(screaming)* No one is ever going to care about you. *(cries deeply, for a long time)*
> (Firestone, 2004, pp. 180-181)

Katie realizes that her mother said similar things to her, and then, in this hypothetical therapy session, Katie says:

> Katie: It's like there's this other person living inside my head. Sometimes it feels like Mom, sometimes though it's like my Dad. Maybe it's both of them, ganged up, trying to kill me. (p. 182)

These considerations lead to several corollaries.

COROLLARY 6a: One useful tactic in psychotherapy is to have the client identify and provide names for their subselves.

Identifying and naming the subselves helps clients recognize, explore, describe, discuss and understand these aspects of themselves. There can be several approaches here. The psychotherapist could encourage a weak form of free association during which the client names and describes the qualities and characteristics of the various subselves. For clients who have difficulties in this process, the psychotherapist could create and provide an inventory of different systems for naming subselves and give illustrations of the names that other clients have found useful.

In Chapter 2, I suggested that it is important for each subself to be recognized, accepted and permitted to have executive control from time to time. To use the concepts of Carl Rogers, we should have unconditional positive regard for each of our subselves. In this way, our entire experience is validated.

COROLLARY 6b: Some subselves are more useful in the psychotherapeutic process than others

The usefulness of particular subselves at particular stages of the psychotherapeutic process is illustrated by crisis intervention. Orton (1974) noted that, in dealing with a client in crisis, it is helpful to get the client's Adult ego state (using Transactional Analysis terminology) in control. If the crisis counselor speaks from a Parent ego state, this will encourage the client to let the Child ego state take over as executive and increase the feelings of helplessness. Asking nonthreatening questions designed to elicit information facilitates the client's Adult ego state assuming executive power and calming the client down.

Theses two corollaries (6a and 6b) are illustrated by the psychotherapy systems proposed by Shapiro and Elliott, by Schwartz, and by Polster.

SHAPIRO AND ELLIOTT

Shapiro and Elliott (1976) noted that we typically talk to ourselves. Inner dialogues take place as conversations between various subselves, different parts of our self with different distinct personal characteristics. Shapiro and Elliott attempted to listen for evidence of conflict in the client during therapy and then tried to separate the different parts of the person involved in this conflict. Shapiro and Elliott saw the psychotherapists's role as that of coach or facilitator, that is, helping the subselves emerge and training the client to deal with them in constructive ways. It is critical that none of the subselves be rejected. Each must be understood and integrated back into the self-organization.

Shapiro and Elliott tried to identify or develop a mediator for the subselves. They called it a chairman of the board, or some term best suited for the particular client. The goal is to transfer energy and power to this mediator (c.f., the ego in psychoanalysis and the Adult ego state in Transactional Analysis). Subself therapy differs from a therapy such as Transactional Analysis because it permits the client to identify and label the subselves, rather than fitting them into a predetermined set of subselves (such as the Child, Adult, and Parent ego states).

Shapiro and Elliott felt that the optimal number of subselves was between four and nine. Too many subselves results in a fragmented or chaotic self and is a form of psychological disturbance. Five kinds of subselves are found in most people:

1. A nurturing parent subself – This self supports and gives love, care, attention, praise, and positive reinforcement.

2   An evaluative parent subself – This self is often called the Critic, Pusher, or Voice of Authority. It reflects the norms and values of the society and sets up standards and measures whether have lived up to them.
3   A central organizing subself – An Executive, Chairman, or Coordinator, who is the self that often works with the Observer and should act as the leader, though it is often displaced by other subselves, such as the Critic.
4   A good, socialized, adapted child subself – This is an obedient, conforming child who tries to please authorities. If this subself is too strong, it can lead to over-conformity, role obedience, and lack of creativity.
5   A natural child subself – This subself is creative, nonconforming, rebellious, spontaneous, and playful.

Subselves can be introjected subselves, especially those that result from identification with a parent. For example, there may be an Audience (or Other People), and there can be internalized parents, such as a Mother.

These subselves can interact in a drama (or life script) as a family, as an organization or task group, or as a discussion group. It is important for the psychological health of the client for the subselves to get along with one another. An internal civil war or great conflict and tension can lead to psychological disturbance. The group of subselves should be democratic, with a minimal amount of partisanship, favoritism, and moralistic judgments. The energy of the subselves should also be rechanneled away from fighting into constructive problem-solving under the leadership of the Chairman. In addition, the Observer should be developed to act as a consultant to the group of subselves.

The Performer versus the Pusher is a common conflict. The Performing Child or Performer is the subself who puts on a performance of some kind, and the Pusher, or Slave Driver, demands that the Performer perform. This often makes the Performer rebel against performing, resulting in conflict. (The Performer may in fact have two subselves, the Socialized Child and the Natural Child.) The Pusher is often associated with a Critic too. In marital conflicts, we often externalize this inner conflict. We project one of our subselves onto the partner and fight with it in the marriage relationship instead of internally. Too great an inner conflict, especially where the Chairman has little power.

Shapiro and Elliott identified several different types of psychopathology:

1   Too many subselves, leading to inner chaos.
2   Too great an inner conflict, especially where the Chairman has little power.

3   Negative emotions (such as sadness and depression) are often caused by one subself attacking the Child, often without the client's awareness.

Psychological health involves having an effective Chairman, who can observe, coordinate and execute decisions, and promote basic harmony among the subselves. However, Shapiro and Elliott noted that integrating the subselves is not enough. We have various subselves, but we are not them. We are greater than the sum of the parts. We have to dis-identify with our subselves eventually, and transcend them. We have to achieve a higher level of awareness – a spiritual harmony that is beyond the psychological harmony.

RICHARD SCHWARTZ

Richard Schwartz (1995) is a psychotherapist who, in talking to clients, realized that they often spoke of different "parts" of themselves.

> Mary: Yeah, I know that I'm doing better, but still I also feel like "Well, why bother?" It's almost an excuse, because then I think I may as well do it [binge and purge], but then I think, "No, I should stop."

> Therapist: It sounds like there are several different parts of you arguing about this. One part is hurt by your parents' lack of recognition and tells you to give up, and another part pushes you to keep trying no matter what they do. Does that sound right? (p. 90)

Schwartz was aware of the work of the other theorists who have proposed a multiplicity of selves, but he preferred to call these subselves "parts," partly because clients can accept and use this term, although he also uses the terms subpersonalities and inner voices. Schwartz estimated that clients typically have between five and fifteen parts. In the case of "Nina," a 27-year-old widow who worked as a personal trainer and who was bulimic, Schwartz identified and labeled seven parts: The Little Girl, Superwoman, The Protector, The Old Lady, The Flower Child, The Barbie Doll and The Monster.

Schwartz noted that it is important to know the "common relationships among a client's network of subpersonalities" (p. 28), that is, the alliances and coalitions that exist and which may change from moment to moment, just as in a family. Indeed, Schwartz viewed the subselves as members of a conflicted family, "alternately protecting and distracting, allying and battling with one another" (p.

32).[12] Over time, during a day, different personalities may take over control of the mind. Some parts have more resources, influence and responsibility. In some people, the parts may become polarized and fight with one another rather than collaborate.

Schwartz labeled some parts as managers, and their task is to control the environment to keeps it safe for the other parts. Other parts can become injured, and then they are isolated and imprisoned by the managers for their own protection – these are called exiles. A third group of parts is made up of the firefighters, parts which stifle and soothe feelings as soon as the exiles become upset.

Schwartz also believed that each person has a "self" (a core self or true self), a core subself that can (and should) and assume leadership of the mind. When the self is in control, the state of mind of the person is uniquely different from the cacophony of voices – a feeling of being centered, calm, light-hearted and confident.

In psychopathological states, the parts fear that the self cannot be an effective leader, and so they protect it. For example, during and after trauma, they may separate the self from the sensations of the body, a process which is called dissociation. In psychotherapy, Schwartz tried to differentiate the self and encourage the parts to place more trust in the self.

ERVING POLSTER

Polster (1995) felt that having a multiplicity of selves (in the present theory, the term is subselves) is preferable to having a single self, but he acknowledges that people are often in search of the a single, essential, real self. This search, however, leads them to reject experiences (both internal and external experiences) that are inconsistent with this real self.

One client, Shelley, was chronically angry, but during one session he realized how hard his life had been. He cried and felt that this new state was the real Shelly, peaceful and soft. However, Polster convinced him that his angry self was an important component of his mind, and that there were perhaps many other selves to be discovered.

---

[12] He also used the analogy of the subselves as parts of an orchestra with the self as the conductor and the analogy of a tribe of people of different ages.

Another defensive tactic is to isolate some of our selves. Certain selves count more than others. In psychotherapy, Polster tries to restore the multiplicity of selves and to ensure that each self is given its rightful place in the group of selves.

Polster noted that selves can be generalized or narrow (such as a depressed self versus a gardening self), culturally (or biologically) universal or idiosyncratic (such as a mothering self versus a coin-collecting self), parallel or interactive (such as doctor self/musician self versus an energetic self/lazy self), and temporary or permanent. More importantly, Polster distinguished between essential selves and member selves. Essential selves are enduring, and individuals experience these selves as part of their" identity." Essential selves can be beneficial for the person or harmful, causing psychological pain. Member selves are more transient and aroused by particular situations.

Henry had felt that he was unintelligent from childhood on. He had a learning disability, and he was unable to achieve his goal (and that of his family for him) of becoming a physician. Henry had become a successful and very rich business man, an achievement which did not diminish his feeling of being stupid. He had many friends and was loved by many people. Polster helped him recognize his beloved self and his successful self, and he helped Henry view them as essential selves rather than member selves. Henry saw his business successes as a result of good luck rather than acumen and skill. By asking detailed questions about each business achievement, Polster helped Henry realize that there was more to his success than luck or fate. Polster took the same approach with Henry's beloved self.

> "He was able to recount many things he had done for people. He had given large bonuses to his employees, he had taken a couple into his home when they were having hard times…He received genuine pleasure from telling me about these acts, as well as from the gratefulness of the recipients…..Attending inwardly to these sensations and realizations……he learned to savor them, and they became more and more real to him." (p. 45).

Transforming Selves

One task in psychotherapy is to transform member selves into essential selves and vice versa. For example, an individual may have a member self that is kind but, if he discovers how pervasive and deeply ingrained his kindness is, he may realize that this is an essential self.

Polster had a depressed public official in therapy, and his many member selves (a competent self, an admired self, a respected self, a determined self) were subservient to an essential self that felt worthless. He managed to deny his worthiness by ascribing people's reactions to him to his superficial personality traits. People liked him because he was clever; they were nice to him because he had power.

At one point in the therapy, he requested an extra appointment, and Polster agreed. When he came, he told Polster that the fact that Polster had given him this extra, special appointment indicated to him that Polster really cared about him. From then on, he began to acknowledge his member selves and to promote them to essential selves. Further therapy revealed that he had a stubborn self that derived from his childhood style with his mother, and a criminal history that he feared others would find out about. If they had, then they would find out that he was not the person they were admiring.

Polster noted that not every personality trait constitutes a member self or an essential self. Rather, only a cluster of personality traits that was evoked in particular situations could constitute a self. Polster also argued that many of the apparent selves that Fritz Perls (Perls, Hefferline & Goodman, 1951) worked with in the "hot-seat" technique of Gestalt Therapy were neither member selves nor essential selves. For example, if a client in Gestalt Therapy uses the two chairs in the hot-seat technique to have a conversation between her left hand and her right hand, this does not necessarily mean that each of these "positions" represent a self. Polster saw them as "momentary players" (p. 49). They merely animate a conversation.

Naming Selves

Identifying and naming the selves can be an important step in psychotherapy. Naming the selves facilitates their recognizability, and the choice of label is critical since the label will have implications. A person who is "careful in his choice of words, noticeably obstructionist about things he is told to do, passive in conversation, and insufficiently interested in his work" (p. 51) might have this self labeled as a who-cares self, a biding-my-time self, a begrudging self, etc, depending on what other traits the person shows. It is important to be accurate in labeling the selves without stigmatizing any of them.

Dialogues between Selves

Polster saw his work with clients who had multiple selves as a form of group therapy. The therapist must interact with each self and also facilitate the communication between the selves.

Polster described the case of Alex, a constructor who had taken on a difficult project which led to conflicts with his client and with those who had urged him to take on the project. He named his multiple selves the naïve self (the self that agreed to take on the project) and the bitter self (the one who was angry at the process). Polster had him alternate the two selves by creating a dialogue between them using the two-chair technique of Gestalt Therapy.

The bitter self became more angry, and the naïve self tried to skirt the issue. Polster urged the naïve self to express his feelings – which turned out to be fear. The client then remembered an incident in his childhood when a boy taunted him and, one day, he lost control and attacked the boy, injuring him. The client then became aware of this dissociated murderous self. Polster helped him to see that he also had a spunky self who had lived under the shadow of the murderous self, and so the client now became aware of and explored four selves.

The naming of selves and, to a lesser extent, the dialogues between them, help to *accentuate* them, spotlights them, and enables the client to experience them more fully. In addition, this helps *orient* the psychotherapist during the process of the therapy.

One client came to recognize that he had an A-student self. He had shunned this self at school because other students saw him as arrogant. He contented himself by merely passing. As an adult, he continued this style – not studying hard enough for licensing exams and stunting his learning process. The result was that he felt as if he were faking his competence and was in danger of being found out to be an impostor. Naming the A-student self accentuated it and encouraged him to accept it and permit it expression in his life.

Comment

For Polster, the end result of therapy could be to merge the selves into one single self, much as Perls tries to do in Gestalt Therapy, but Polster thought that it was preferable to retain all the selves, even the dissonant selves, to have them co-exist, creating a point-counterpoint, much like a flower arrangement or an orchestra. Sacrificing some selves in the service of coherence leads to personal distortion, a most undesirable state of affairs.

COROLLARY 6c: A useful technique for helping clients recognize, explore and alleviate conflict between their subselves is the "empty chair" technique used in Gestalt therapy.

The client can situate different subselves in the chairs and create a dialogue between them. For clients who prefer, a written dialogue between subselves can be created in a journal (Progoff, 1975). Clients can be encouraged to use diaries to document where and when different subselves assume executive power, their characteristics and the situations in which they assume control. For those who are comfortable with computer programs such as EXCEL, spreadsheets could be created to assist this process for easy entry of the data.

From an existential viewpoint, clients can be encouraged to explore the meaning of each subself. What purpose does each subself serve? How authentic is each subself? Why do particular subselves appear in certain situations? What is needed or confronted in that situation that a particular subself can provide?

COROLLARY 6d: Subselves may act to preserve an individual's self-esteem by viewing their undesirable characteristics as merely one subself.

If a client has a problem such as depression, low self-esteem, perfectionism, an eating disorder or an addiction, by viewing this aspect of the self as a separate subself, the problem does not "label" the whole person. Instead of viewing oneself as a depressed person, for example, one can conceptualize oneself as a complex individual with one subself that is depressed.

Clients could explore and describe the "negative" aspects of themselves and then label this as a separate subself with a name. Whenever clients experience these negative thoughts, desires and emotions, they can think, "Oh, that's my xxx subself again." Clients may already possess another subself that is antithetical to this negative subself and which can challenge it. If not, the psychotherapist can help clients develop new, healthy subselves that can challenge the negative subself.

MINDFULNESS MEDITATION

In mindfulness mediation, the individuals are instructed to be aware of any and all mental content, including thoughts, images, physical sensation and emotions as they occur to them on a moment-by-moment basis. This content is not to be evaluated or judged. No labels are to be applied such as good versus bad or healthy versus sick. The content is simply to be observed and registered. In true Zen Buddhist fashion - what is, is; what isn't, isn't.

Birnbaum and Birnbaum (2004) have pointed out that mindfulness meditation requires the development of an observing self, which is very similar to the recording secretary in Shapiro and Elliott's system of psychotherapy. The observing self is also developed in cognitive therapy when clients are instructed to observe their irrational thoughts and to keep a log in which they record them, note the antecedent and then change the irrational thought to a rational thought. Of course, whereas cognitive therapy encourages the challenging of the irrational thoughts, mindfulness requires simply observing them. In mindfulness meditation, the content of the mind is not challenged, but people's attitude or relationship to the content is changed.

SUGGESTIONS FROM FAMILY THERAPY

If the mind can be viewed as consisting of a set of subselves, then the principles of group therapy (Yalom, 1995) and family therapy (Gladding, 2007) may provide useful concepts and tactics for conducting individual psychotherapy.

COROLLARY 6e: It is important in psychotherapy to know the relationships among a client's network of subselves, that is, the alliances and coalitions that exist and how they change from time to time and situation to situations.

COROLLARY 6f: Some subselves may become enmeshed, and the psychotherapist must help the client create sufficiently impermeable boundaries. Alternatively, some subselves may become disengaged, and the task then is to recognize them and encourage them to express themselves.

Corollaries 6e and 6f come from ideas common in family therapy (e.g., Minuchin, 1974). Family therapy recognizes that the person who has the "problem" is not necessarily the problem person in the family. Rather, the whole family is the problem, and the designated disturbed family member is simply the scapegoat for the family. Family therapy focuses on the family system and the changes than can be made in that system. The psychotherapist's "client" is the whole family, and the psychotherapist's goal is to change the whole family, rather than hoping that a change in one member of the family as a result of individual psychotherapy will have repercussions on the other family members.

There many approaches for the family therapist to choose from. Jackson and Weakland (1961) focused on the communication networks in the family, the expectations that each family member has for the other family members, the social roles of each family member, and the implicit rules that the family members have set up for one another. Haley (1971) focused on the power struggles that occur in families and also on the levels of communication where the words spoken by a family member may be contradicted by the tone of voice or body language.

Bowen (1971) suggested that family sometimes develop an undifferentiated family-ego mass, that is, a quality of "stick-togetherness" in which the individual family members have not developed clear and distinct concepts of themselves. People who are undifferentiated focus on their feelings, and these feelings are determined in large part by those around them. Bowen endeavored to get the individual family members to differentiate themselves from the fused family. The family members must become more inner-directed, establishing their own goals and deciding upon their own behaviors.

Applying these concepts to the multiple self theory of personality, the goals of the therapist should identify (1) any communication difficulties between the various subselves (and develop useful new subselves such as recording secretaries and mediators), (2) the power struggles between the subselves, (3) the coalitions that have formed between the subselves, and (4) the degree to which the subselves have developed clear identities and firm boundaries so as to prevent becoming enmeshed or undifferentiated.

FIXED-ROLE THERAPY

George Kelly (1955), as part of his theory of personal constructs, proposed a therapy which he called fixed-role therapy. Having identified the constructs which the client uses to construe the world, the therapist constructs a new role for the client to try. This new role is given a different name from that of the client, and the client is encouraged to try this new role on occasions.

Viney (1981) has provided an example. Her client was an attractive, intelligent young woman in her 20s who experienced a great deal of anxiety, which in Kelly's theory indicates that her construction system did not help her make sense of or understand the events that she was experiencing. The client also experienced shame (about living at home, not being attractive and still being a virgin). As a result, the client built a wall around herself to distance herself from others.

Viney elicited her constructs and then constructed a role for her to try out. This new role, called Mary Jones, was a friendly woman who is open and frank with others. Mary enjoyed giving to others and feeling companionship with them. Mary was down-to-earth and relaxed most of the time, patient with others and not critical of them. She was also inquisitive and forceful if need be. Viney found that the client was able to try out this new role in some situations and, as a result, her construct system changed in the direction of this new role.

Fixed-role therapy, therefore, is odd. In seeking to help clients, it encourages suppression of one subself and seeks to substitute a new subself. Kelly and other personal construct therapists do not give clear guidelines as to how the psychotherapist should construct this new role. In some ways, it represents an ideal self and is often the opposite of the self that the client has presented to the psychotherapist. Viney's client built a wall around herself to distance herself from others, and the new role thrust her into interacting with and trusting others in a relaxed manner.

Fixed-role psychotherapists always deny that they want the client to "be" this new subself. "At no stage did either of us intend that she become Mary Jones" (Viney, 1981, p. 275). Despite this denial, fixed-role therapy does seem to encourage the development of a new subself for the client. For example, Bonarius (1970) said, ".....if you can be James you might also be able to play the other characters" (p. 213). "If I act in a different way I can be different. I can be different from what I think I am. I can change" (p. 213). Although Bonarius states that the goal of fixed-role therapy is "not for the client permanently to exchange his own personality for that of the role character" (p. 217), the fixed-role therapist is actively trying "to make the patient develop a new system" (p. 218).

It is possible that clients may use the feedback obtained while playing the role suggested by the psychotherapist to modify their existing construction system while keeping it as one unified whole. On the other hand, especially if the client already has several subselves, fixed role therapy may encourage the development of a new subself.

MULTIPLE SELF THERAPY[13]

The first stage is of multiple self therapy psychoeducational in nature.[14] Unlike systems of psychotherapy such as psychoanalysis (the knowledge of which

---

[13] This section was co-authored by Thomas J. Rankin and Nick Joyce.
[14] The stages can be briefly summarized as psychoeducational, identification, action, and termination.

is widespread in our culture) or cognitive therapy which has been written about extensively in self-help books and magazines, clients will not have heard of multiple self theory, and so they will need an introduction to the idea. This requires homework readings for clients so that they can maximize their time in the sessions and the length of the overall psychotherapy. It would be useful to prepare pamphlets to describe multiple self theory for clients.

From a constructivist point of view, it is important that the psychotherapist creates a shared understanding with clients about their worldview. First, the psychotherapist needs to know whether clients see themselves as having a multiple self or a single self. Clients could then be asked to give some examples of their subselves and to write down all the possible subselves that they might have. The ease of this task will vary from client to client. Some clients have subselves that they can easily identify. Other clients may have subselves, but it may take time for them to figure out what they are. It may help to have clients think about other people that they know and identify the subselves in those individuals. Identifying subselves in others may help clients recognize their own subselves. To raise the issue of executive control, the psychotherapist could ask: "Right now, which subself would you say is in charge?" "Which subself is usually in charge?" "How long does any one subself tend to stay in control?"

The psychotherapist and the client could work together to paint a picture of how the client's subselves interact. The client could be encouraged to think whether any subselves work together, form coalitions or are at odds with one another. The use of diaries (and spreadsheets), as noted above, may assist clients in exploring their subselves. If clients have trouble understanding and applying the concept of subselves, the psychotherapist can switch to using roles as a conduit to understanding subselves. "What roles do you have in your life? Parent, teacher, leader, follower?" After exploring the roles in which the clients engage on a regular basis, clients can be encouraged to name their subselves for the roles that they control. Clients' independence and engagement in psychotherapy can be encouraged by making sure that the clients provide names for their subselves, thereby taking ownership of the structure of their personality.

The psychotherapist must also determine whether the subselves contaminate (or intrude into) one another (or are enmeshed). The subselves should have firm boundaries, and this task may be facilitated by having the client identify and describe each of the subselves. The empty chair technique to create dialogues between subselves may also help the formation of form boundaries.

The problems presented by clients might help shape the number and names of their subselves. For example, if client feel anxious because they cannot decide how to prioritize their tasks (as in a generalized anxiety disorder), clients can first be encouraged to conceptualize this state as a subself. Then the psychotherapist can ask them, "If you were to have a decisive subself, what would it be like?" Clients can then be encouraged to develop this decisive subself to act as a counterbalance to the indecisive and anxious subself.

This technique can also be used for moods. If the client has a depressed subself, the psychotherapist can explore whether the client has a happy subself and how this happy subself can be developed as a counterbalance to the depressed self. Likewise, for anxious subselves traumatized subselves, child-like subselves, angry subselves, and so on. Complementary subselves could be developed for each – a calm subself, a parental subself, and so on. This process can be strange, difficult and even frightening. Clients will eventually begin to utilize these subselves and let them assume executive control outside of the psychotherapy sessions.

For example, if the psychotherapist has a client who struggles with shame, the client could be asked, "Where are some safe places that you can let the subselves of which you are ashamed emerge?" The client can be encouraged to reflect on whether that subself is really shameworthy or if, instead, the client simply fears that others will disapprove of that subself's voice. Question such as, "What would happen if you let the shameful subself emerge in public?" might explore the fears and the consequences that the client wishes to avoid. Behaviorally, the client could be encouraged to experiment with letting the shameful subself take executive control with people that the client trusts or in situations where the consequences would be minor (as is the case in the psychotherapy sessions). Through such experiments, clients might discover that the subself is not as shameworthy and does not produce the negative consequences that they feared.

Clients and psychotherapists can work together to see what function each subself serves and how each subself contributes to the individual's success. The therapeutic alliance could be built and strengthened by jointly brainstorming ways in which existing subselves might take over the functions of subselves that cause friction or problems. If necessary, new subselves can be created whose function it is to minimize confusion among the subselves, to mediate between the subselves or to lead the subselves. Looking to past experience can be helpful here. "Have you ever eliminated or minimized a subself? How? Could you do that again? Which subself might take over the beneficial functions of the troublesome subself?"

Clients can be encouraged to reflect on how their subselves interact. Clients might be told: "Often, people try to make one coherent or consistent sense of themselves by establishing a pecking order or stable coalitions (or other ways of structuring their subselves); how do you do this? If you don't, how could you?"

Psychotherapists and their clients could brainstorm together about the various ways that the clients' subselves might be ordered – as a small, harmonious, co-existing group of subselves or with a dominant chief executive who decides which subself will be front and center at any time. Discussions about childhood experiences or past successes are relevant here. "When have you been successful in the past? Which subselves were responsible for that success? What was the relationship between your subselves at that time? How could you duplicate that in the future?"

After the psychotherapist and client have explored the types, names and structure among the client's subselves, the psychotherapist might bring up the idea of real (or core) versus façade selves. The psychotherapist could ask, "Which of your subselves feels like the 'real you' and which exist just to satisfy the demands that others make on you?" (These two polarities are not always mutually exclusive since a client could have a subself that both is focused on satisfying the needs of others but which also feels central or 'real' to himself.) However, such a probe might start a useful conversation that sheds light on which subselves the client experiences as false or troubling.

Another avenue to explore would be the origin of the various subselves. The psychotherapist can ask: "Which subselves go back the furthest in time? Are there any you remember from your childhood or adolescence?" and "How do the views and attitudes of your parents map onto any of your subselves. How did your parents shaped and mold your subselves?" Eventually, the psychotherapist might come to feel that the client should have outgrown one or more of the subselves, but at first it is important to learn about their origin. While some subselves from childhood may still be useful for the client, others may no longer be useful. Identifying these childlike subselves can help clients to identify the parts of themselves that they would like to modify.

Clients can be asked to identify people that they particularly admire or the traits of others that they would like to emulate. A client could create and name a new subself after the admired other. Alternatively, the psychotherapist could ask, "How could you incorporate aspects of the admired person's personality into your subselves?"

The focus throughout is on client empowerment and utilizing subselves to provide a schema by which individual can create a system for understand their experience of themselves. Though many closed-ended questions were proffered above, broad open-ended questions can also foster adult, competent behavior by the client as opposed to the client adopting a childlike subself in response to a domineering psychotherapist whose "expertise" is going to safely parent the client to personal growth. By challenging the client's experience of themselves as one unified whole, encouraging instead a nuanced view in which the experience of the self changes as various subselves emerge and exert influence on the person, the client would be freed to make changes that he or she desires.

Rather than having to change the 'entire self,' which might seem like an insurmountable task, clients have only to identify those subselves that are no longer functioning well and either minimize (or suspend) them or change them, or create new subselves that will help them to function as they wish to. As constructivist psychotherapists, psychotherapists must continually check to make certain that they are not imposing their own worldview on the client. "Do you find the notion of subselves useful? Is it helping?" But, in truth, a psychotherapist using any system of psychotherapy must ensure that the client understands the system that is being used and that the client accepts the view of that system.

DISCUSSION

The following passage from Minuchin (1974, p. 54)) is phrased in terms of family functioning, but it could easily be re-written for multiple self functioning:

> For proper family functioning, the boundaries of subsystems must be clear. They must be defined well enough to allow subsystem members to carry out their functions without undue interference, but they must allow contact between members of the subsystem and others. The composition of subsystems organized around family functions is not nearly as significant as the clarity of subsystem boundaries.

It is clear the multiple self theory of personality has many implications for psychotherapy. Some systems of psychotherapy, such an Jung's Analytic Psychology and Berne's Transactional Analysis, already use the notion of subselves, and new systems have been proposed based more clearly on the concept of subselves (such as Shapiro and Elliott and Polster). The multiple self theory of personality may well stimulate further thought on the possible tactics for the effective psychotherapy of individuals.

Chapter 7

MULTIPLE SELF THEORY, DISSOCIATION AND REINCARNATION/POSSESSION

> Anger and tenderness: my selves.
> And now I can believe they breathe in me
> As angels, not polarities.
>
> (Adrienne Rich, 1981, p. 9)

There are many phenomena which lend themselves to a multiple self explanation and in this chapter we will explore some of them, including multiple personality, possession, mediums who communicate with the dead, reincarnation, and hallucinations. The hypothesis will be proposed that these phenomena fall on a dimension of dissociation, that is, the degree to which the subself is accepted or rejected as a part of the self.

MULTIPLE PERSONALITY

At one extreme is multiple personality (officially known as dissociative identity disorder) in which the individual has two or more personalities (subpersonalities or alternate personalities), each of which has its own set of memories, thoughts, emotions and behaviors. In dramatic cases, the different subpersonalities have no awareness of one another (mutually amnesic), in some cases subpersonalities may be aware of the others but the awareness is not mutual (one-way amnesia), while in other cases they may be aware of one another and even converse (mutually cognizant). The different subpersonalities of the person with multiple personality may be conceptualized in the present theory as subselves, and the goal of psychotherapy typically is to merge or fuse these different subselves into a single integrated self.

POSSESSION

Possession is a belief system in a culture (or subculture) that the person has been possessed by some other "personality" (Bourguignon, 1976) which is used to explain certain behavior by people. When people are possessed, according to this belief, they can be said to be an in a "possession trance" or a possession state (Bourguignon, 1976). This state usually involves changes in consciousness and often affects the behavior of the possessed person.

Depending upon the cultural beliefs, this state can be involuntary, harmful and undesirable, in which case the person or his relatives often turn to a shaman in order to exorcize the spirit possessing the individual. However, the possessing entity can be seen as desirable, as in American Pentecostal religious groups, the members of which, after possession by the Holy Ghost, speak in tongues *(glossolalia)* or as in mediums who sometimes become possessed during their sessions (Firth, 1969). Finally, in some societies, the initial possession is viewed as deviant, but efforts are made to control the possession -- to domesticate it (Bourguignon, 1976).

Ward (1980) distinguished between *ritual possession* which is voluntary, reversible and short-term, supported by cultural beliefs, induced by engaging in ritual ceremonies and irrelevant to cultural concepts of illness, and *peripheral possession* which is involuntary and long-term, viewed negatively by the culture, and constitutes a pathological reaction in the individual.

Pattison and Wintrob (1981) saw possession as spanning a continuum from concrete (that is, with a high degree of *personification and specification)* at one end to abstract (that is, possession by thoughts, impulses, memories or images) at the other. Their taxonomy included (1) trance, an altered state of consciousness which is a culturally-learned pattern of behavior, (2) possession trance, with possession by and impersonation of another being, (3) neurotic possession behavior, a syndrome involving unusual, idiosyncratic, deviant, aberrant or pathological behavior which can be interpreted as the result of possession, and (4) psychotic possession behavior, involving culture-bound syndromes such as amok and wiitiko, involving psychotic behavior.

Pattison and Wintrob gave an example of possession behavior involving culture-conflict resolution.

A Mexican girl who was engaged, received word that her fiancé had died in an accident. She had not wanted to marry the man and was relieved to escape the marriage but her family had wanted the marriage to solidify village social ties and saw the death as a severe social loss. The girl began to complain of nightmares and nightly visitations by her fiancé, who possessed her. A *brujo* was consulted and he performed a ritual of exorcism. The *brujo* placed each family member in magic circles to protect them. He invited the ghost into the house, explained to him that he was now dead and needed to leave the girl and to go to his proper place with dead people. He explained that the ghost would be missed, but this was the natural order. The ghost was dismissed out the door. The symptoms of the girl rapidly subsided. (p. 16)

In Brazil, a transplanted tradition from the Yoruba in Nigeria is called candomblé, in which each participant of the cult has a guardian spirit or "orixa" which can possess the person during trance states (Csordas, 1987). In Zaire, people who contract the Zebola illness, which is the result of possession, enter the Zebola community, and the religious rituals encourage the possessing spirit to help the person rather than harm her (Corin, 1979). In South Kanara in southern India, there is a Siri cult whose members believe that young girls can be possessed by one of five Siri who are the deceased spirits from one family from the past (Claus, 1979).[15] The girl now becomes a medium and can be possessed by the spirit when she desires it rather than the spirit having control over the times of possession. In these three societies, the religious cult gives the participants power over their possessing spirits and enables them to have control over the spirits.

Krippner (1987) reported on the belief in possession in Brazil where there are three traditional spiritism sects: Candomblé, Kardecismo, and Umbanda. Spirit possession is used to explain what people in the West would label obsessive thoughts, multiple personality, epilepsy and schizophrenia. Sometimes, the spirit which is possessing the person is thought to be one from a previous life of the person, that is, a reincarnated spirit. Krippner reported a case of a girl who in her teens acted like a tomboy and was upset when she developed a female physique. The explanation of the Brazilian mediums was that she had been a boy in a previous life, and this male personality had taken possession of the girl's mind.

Krippner reported the case of Sonia, an 18-year-old girl in Brazil who had one-night stands with men, without achieving orgasm. She sometimes fought with these men but had no memory of this afterwards. She had been treated with medications and electroconvulsive therapy. With the mediums, she began to speak in French and claimed to be Violetta from the 18th Century. Violetta was

---

[15] The process by which a deceased person becomes a spirit is called apotheosis.

promiscuous and wanted to possess Sonia's body even more completely. The mediums tried to limit Violetta's power and to synthesize her desires with those of Sonia. After six treatments, the personalities were merged, and Sonia was able to have orgasms. Sonia had achieved greater self-awareness and self-control. At that point, another personality emerged, Sarah, a Jewish housewife from the 16th Century, a personality which was more mature than Sonia or Violetta, followed by Chen, a Chinese male. Sonia recalled "meeting" all three personalities when she was a child and considered them to be her spirit playmates. It took eighteen months of treatment to merge these personalities. No effort was made to explore the reality of the existence of the three personalities from earlier times. Interestingly, Sonia developed spots on her body during her possession by Sarah which corresponded to burns Sarah had received when she was burned (and killed) at the stake. The spots disappeared after two days.

The possessing agent can be a God, the Devil, an unknown dead spirit, or a known dead spirit. Possessing spirits can be from your former life or from someone else's life; they can be a non-human "low" spirit, or they can be the spirit of someone still alive (such as a sorcerer). Sometimes the possessing spirit is encouraged to leave the person (and occasionally exorcised), while sometimes it is merged with the host personality. Occasionally, a person may retain the spirit which is possessing them and become a medium.

Interestingly, anthropologists (and the mediums they observe) who report such cultural cases are not interested in the truth or possibility of fraud in the spirit presentation (Firth, 1969). They are interested in whether the behaviors produced are consciously produced or unconsciously produced and what cultural function possession serves, such as novelty, an outlet for esthetics (as in dancing), and treatment for those who are sick.

Varma, et al. (1981) speculated that cases of possession were similar to cases of multiple personality. They noted that cases of possession were very common in India, whereas cases of multiple personality were rare. Cases of possession in India last from a few hours to a few weeks, but the people remain conscious of their surroundings and their true identity during the experience. They are also aware of prior possessions when they are back in their normal states, that is, they do not have amnesia. In these respects, possession states are very different from multiple personality. Interestingly, possession is found, not only in Hindus, who believe in reincarnation, but in Muslims in India, who do not.

Possession in Psychiatric Patients

Goff, et al. (1991) has noted that possession is often claimed by psychiatric patients. In a sample of sixty-one patients with chronic psychotic disorders, 41 percent claimed to have been or to be currently possessed. Those claiming possession did not differ in sex or age from those who not make such a claim, but they had more often been sexually abused as children (though not more often physically abused), to have used cannabis and to have auditory hallucinations. Goff did not ask about the identity of the possessing spirit, but the implication of Goff's research is that the belief that one is possessed is a symptom of severe psychiatric disorder and is a symptom similar to other dissociative disorders, such as multiple personality and psychologically-induced amnesia.

Iida (1989), working in Japan, saw possession as a delusional state and documented its incidence and characteristics in psychiatric patients. He found that 21 percent of the patients had this symptom. The most common agent was a God, but possessions by spirits, humans and animals were also reported. Possession was more common in schizophrenic patients and in younger patients.

Yap (1960) felt that the syndrome could serve the purposes of attempts at wish fulfillment, dramatization and working-through guilt conflicts, and manipulation of others. One woman patient had been told by evangelists visiting her in hospital that her tuberculosis was a result of her sin and that she could be cured only if the Holy Ghost possessed her. She soon became "possessed" by Jesus and another obscure God and was treated with sedation and psychotherapy.

Bull (2001) noted that some patients with multiple personality occasionally report that some of the "personalities" are alien to them, and they feel possessed. In these cases, Bull suggested that an exorcism, carried out in the custom of the patient's religion or folk philosophy, can be a useful adjunct to the psychotherapy. The exorcism should never be forced on the patient and used only for the personality (or personalities) that the patient labels as alien. The remaining personalities can then be integrated into the person's psyche using more traditional therapeutic tactics.

Comments

Kenny (1981) noted that some scholars view possession, spirits talking through mediums (particularly those who go into a trance while mediating between the spirit world and our world) and multiple personality as similar phenomena. Thus, attempts are occasionally made to explain one of the phenomena by viewing it as a case of the others. Multiple personalities could be the result of possession; possession could be a type of multiple personality. Richeport (1992) noted that people with multiple personalities and those possessed by spirits usually make good subjects for hypnosis, and both of these phenomena can, supposedly, be induced by hypnosis (and, it might be added, be faked by the people).

From the point of view the theory of personality proposed in this book, it is likely that the "spirits" which apparently possess individuals are one of their subselves which has taken over control of the mind.[16]

COMMUNICATION WITH DEAD SPIRITS

Spiritualism is a Christian religion whose beliefs include the idea that the spirits of deceased persons move to a spirit world and that it is possible to communicate with the deceased spirits occasionally through living persons called *mediums*.

Although in movies, mediums often go into trances and speak in the voice of the deceased person and, occasionally, apparitions appear, this is quite uncommon. In Great Britain, where Spiritualism is an organized religion with an organized bureaucracy, almost no mediums behave in this way. The medium and visitors typically sit in comfortable chairs, and the medium passes on messages to the visitors while in a normal psychological state. She may say, "I have an Elizabeth here who wants to communicate. Does anyone here know an Elizabeth?" After establishing that the spirit is known, the medium may pass on a message. "She wants me to tell you that......"

Spiritualism has various uncodified beliefs which may vary with the particular sect or group. The British beliefs typically include a negative view of suicide (the spirits of those who commit suicide go into a type of limbo, and mediums advise against suicide), the notion that those who die suddenly are disoriented on the other side and have to rest for while before moving on, and that there are several levels in the spirit world ranging from the squalid to the sumptuous. Those who have been evil during their earthly life are sent to the lower realms, a kind of hell.

Unfortunately, occasional mediums in the past have been frauds, and the existence of even one fraud creates doubt about all mediums. For example, a

---

[16] In an analogous manner, the "it" that comes over us and makes us behave in socially unacceptable ways was construed by Freud as originating in the individual's own id.

modern medium has been suspected of fraud. Jaroff (2001) reported on John Edward, a medium whose shows appear on cable television, and noted the ways in which Edward might obtain information about the people to whom he gives "readings," ranging from clues they give as they respond to his guesses, to information they provide to his assistants prior to shows. One participant saw that the televised show had edited out the guesses that Edward had made which were wrong and spliced in shots of him nodding in agreement to guesses which he remembered disagreeing with. This participant also suspected that hidden microphones might have picked up clues while the participants were kept waiting for long periods of time.

Some people find it more easy to believe in extrasensory perception than in life after death. Thus, when a medium communicates information from a supposedly deceased person's spirit, it is possible to argue that the medium is picking up information from living people, present or absent, via extrasensory perception and passing this information on. This seems to be a more parsimonious explanation of the phenomenon.

Mediums who communicate with the dead often have a spirit guide (also known as a control) who passes on messages from deceased individuals intended for those who have come to the medium for such messages (Lester, 2005). Occasional mediums are "possessed" by the deceased spirit and speak as if they "are" the deceased person. Commentators have noted the similarity of this phenomenon to the psychiatric syndrome of multiple personality. Thus, the "spirit" could be dissociated part of the medium's own mind. However, it is interesting to note that multiple personality involves amnesia. One personality has no memory of what takes place during the other personality's domination of the individual's mind. It is not always the case that mediums have amnesia.

From the point of view of subself theory, controls may be subselves of the mediums which they do not recognize as such, a possibility first suggested over a hundred years ago by Flournoy (1900).

REINCARNATION MEMORIES[17]

Reincarnation is a phenomenon in which, after a person dies, the soul or spirit survives and waits for a period of time before entering the body of newly conceived baby. This baby then possesses memories of some of the life experiences of the previous person from which the soul or spirit came.

---

[17] For a recent review of research into reincarnation, see Lester (2005).

Reincarnation then, if it can be proven, would provide strong evidence for life after death.

The major researcher into reincarnation is Ian Stevenson. Stevenson (1977) has collected many hundreds of reports of reincarnation, often personally interviewing the people involved. He describes the typical case as follows. A child, two to six years old, begins to tell his parents about a previous existence. The child may show unusual behavior from the point of view of his family, but this behavior later proves to be consistent with the previous existence. The child asks to be taken to the place where he lived previously, and his family tries to identify the previous incarnation. The search for the previous family is successful, and the child is found to be correct and accurate in about 90 percent of the statements he made about the previous existence. After the age of five or six, the child talks less about the previous existence, and his memories fade.

Stevenson (1977) reported that he and his colleagues had collected more than 1,600 such reports, mainly from India, Sri Lanka, Burma and Thailand, Turkey, Lebanon, Syria, and northwest America. These are regions and cultures where the inhabitants believe in reincarnation. Reports from Europe and much of America, where belief in reincarnation is rare, tend to be less numerous and poorer in quality.

Objections

There have been many objections made about the "reality" of reincarnation reports. Thouless (1984) has objected to some reincarnation memories as being too "good." One subject, for example, reported days of the week when events occurred in previous lives, as well as the year, whereas Thouless could not remember such details for early events in his own life.

Stevenson (1988) has documented many cases of deception and self-deception in claims of reincarnation. In one case of an Israeli for whom it was claimed he spoke ancient Hebrew dating from the time of King David, Stevenson decided that the journalist who first reported the case had invented the case. In other cases, Stevenson was able to finds details suggesting that villagers had consciously deceived investigators, hoping for some reward for having one of their children being a reincarnation of some particular person.

In addition to fraud, there are also incompetent investigators. In the famous case of Bridey Murphy (Bernstein, 1956), Virginia Tighe, a housewife in Pueblo, Colorado, was hypnotized by Morey Bernstein and began to recall an existence in Ireland as Bridey Murphy. The book on the case became a best-seller, but even a superficial investigation would have revealed (and eventually did reveal) that the "facts" recalled by Mrs. Tighe could all be found to stem from childhood experiences in Chicago where she lived across the street from a woman whose maiden name was Bridie Murphy (Gardner, 1957). This type of case is not so much a fraud as a result of incompetence on the part of the investigators.[18]

A common objection raised against reported cases of reincarnation is cryptomnesia. In cryptomnesia, the persons learns and remembers information about a dead person but later forgets the source of the information and the fact that he or she ever obtained it. Thus, it is also called *source amnesia*. Cryptomnesia can be called upon to explain all kinds of data which suggest life before and after death, as well as such phenomena as *déjà vu* and unintentional plagiarism.

An example of cryptomnesia is given by Kampman and Hirvenoja (1978). A Finnish girl of about twelve was regressed during hypnosis to eight previous lives, including one as an English girl called Dorothy who lived in the Middle Ages. This girl sang a medieval song. Seven years later, under hypnosis, she remembered that she had seen the song in the Finnish translation of a book of English songs, a book which could be traced.

Some have suggested that reincarnation "memories" are the result of paranormal interactions among living people, in particular, supernormal extra-sensory perception and clairvoyance. Anderson (1985) however, has noted that there is little evidence for such "super-esp." If instead, such supernormal paranormal powers are credited to the deceased person (who communicates with the living via esp) rather than credited to the living, then these spirits display powers in death that they did not possess in life. Anderson also suggested that it would be impossible to provide evidence to support either of these explanations.

Some commentators have suggested that recalling previous existences is a psychiatric symptom, and so people who do so are psychiatrically disturbed. There are instances where a person who is psychiatrically disturbed claims to have been reincarnated. For example, Pasricha, et al. (1978) described a man who was psychotic, probably schizophrenic, who during one interview talked about a previous life. After his recovery, he never made such claims again. However, not all those recalling previous existences are psychiatrically disturbed.

Other explanations include that the person is simply daydreaming and fantasizing, that reincarnation memories are products of the Jungian collective unconscious (explanations which would not explain the accuracy of reported

---

[18] Commentators still disagree on whether the "facts" revealed in this case could have been "learned" by Virginia Tighe in the course of her life.

memories of a previous existence), and that the reincarnation report is a result of "paramnesia" in which the person's family and the family of the previous incarnation have met and inadvertently exchanged information (an explanation which would not explain situations in which the two families never meet).

Reincarnation or Possession?

Stevenson and Story (1970) reported the case of Disna, born in 1959 in a small village in Sri Lanka. When she was three years old, Disna spontaneously reported experiences from a previous existence which took place in a village three-and-a-half miles away. In response to questions, she revealed more information, but she showed no desire to visit the village. Her family persuaded her to visit the village in 1964, and she seemed to recognize the place and to reveal accurate knowledge, such as entering the home there by the same door which her previous personality, Babanona, had used, a woman who had died in 1958, fifteen months before Disna was born.

Stevenson and his colleagues investigated the case in 1965 and again in 1968, at which times Disna still remembered the details, although she had ceased to refer to her previous existence spontaneously. Stevenson noted that the two families knew each other casually – to recognize one another on the road if they passed. They never had any social acquaintance and had not entered each other's houses. The two families did, however, have two mutual acquaintances.

Disna reported 34 facts about her previous existence, and 33 of these were verified by informants. The details were so extensive that Stevenson felt that the identification of the previous personality was quite unambiguous, for example, that Babanona had travelled by car and train to visit relatives in a specific town.

Disna made 15 statements indicating recognition of people and places in Babanona's life, and she was correct in 14 of these. In addition, Disna showed several personality traits similar to Babanona, such as religiousness and antagonism toward Babanona's son. She also showed similar skills, such as being able to weave coconut leaves when she was only three years old. Disna differed from other cases, according to Stevenson, in her reluctance to visit the home village of Babanona and in that she reported that her previous life had been unhappy.

Stevenson felt that fraud was unlikely in this case, and he was unable to find evidence that Disna had acquired this information from visitors to her home. Extrasensory perception could not be ruled out, except that Disna appeared to have no other type of paranormal abilities. Thus, possession and reincarnation remained the most likely explanations for the case.

As we can see, it is often very hard to distinguish cases of reincarnation from cases of possession. However, from the perspective of subself theory, both may be situations where subselves take over the control of the mind temporarily, what Jung (1977) called split-off or secondary personalities. Woolger (1988), who uses past-life exploration as a therapeutic technique, remained uncertain as to whether memories of past lives are proof of regression or aspects of the person's real self. He suggested that, "these characters from previous eras are recognizable as *other selves,* that we dimly know have always been there in the background of our consciousness" (p. 15).

HALLUCINATIONS

Schizophrenics often have auditory hallucinations in which they hear voices. Typically the schizophrenics attribute these voices to some external agency, but the voices most likely originate in their own minds and may be conceptualized as coming from other subselves.

Van Dusen (1973) approached several psychiatric patients and told them that he wanted to get an accurate description of their experiences. He wanted to get in touch with the hallucinations, and even talk with the voices that his patients heard. His patients knew that their experiences were not shared by others. They were often embarrassed by what they heard and saw, and Van Dusen took pains to make them comfortable enough to reveal their experiences to him. His patients seemed to be fairly sensible people who were as puzzled as he was by their experiences.

Van Dusen found that most of his patients thought that they had contact with another world or order of beings, for most part other living persons. All objected to the term "hallucination." They coined their own terms instead, such as "The other order" or "The eavesdroppers." For most, the hallucinations came on suddenly, and most were frightened and had difficulty adjusting to this new experience. They soon realized that no one else heard these voices or shared these experiences, and so they kept them to themselves.

Van Dusen discovered two kinds of voices.

1   Lower order voices were like drunken bums who teased, tormented and abused the patients. They insulted them, suggested lewd and immoral acts

and made threats. For example, one patient heard voices plotting his death, while others were shouted at constantly by dozens of voices.

2   Higher order hallucinations were supportive, less often involved voices and were more symbolic. The man who heard voices plotting his death had a light come to him one night, like a sun. When he approached this friendly sun, he found himself in a corridor with doors behind which raged the powers of hell. As he was about open one of the doors and let the powers out, he was approached by a Christ-like figure who counseled him to leave the doors closed and to follow him.

In his essay, Van Dusen compared these accounts of his patients to the world of spirits described by Emanuel Swedenborg (1688-1772). Swedenborg, while living a productive life in the world, had daily intercourse with spirits which he wrote about in his religious books. Swedenborg's description of the spirit world had many parallels with the descriptions given by Van Dusen's patients, and this was made more remarkable because Van Dusen's patients were talking to Van Dusen independently of one another yet gave similar accounts.

What is of interest here is that Van Dusen wondered whether hallucinations are detached pieces of the patients' unconscious or possession by spirits. Or are these two alternatives simply two ways of describing the same process? Van Dusen's question reminded me of visiting my mother many years ago, who was a member of the Spiritualist Association in England and who attended Spiritualist church meetings. At that time, there was famous medium, a young man in his twenties who was sought after for sittings in which he would pass on messages from deceased loved ones to his sitters. He had begun to hear voices in his adolescence, and his parents, spiritualists, had viewed this as an ability to communicate with spirits. They trained him so that, ten years later, he was a successful medium. I realized that, had he born into a different family, his parents would have taken him to a psychiatrist who would have diagnosed him as a schizophrenic, and he would have become a psychiatric patient.

In the present context, hallucinations are seen as dissociated subselves, just as the spirits who communicate with mediums are.

A CLINICAL CASE

Lubchansky, Egri and Stokes (1970) described the case of a 15-year-old girl in Puerto Rico who would get into violent arguments with her father , after which she would wander the streets without being aware of her identity or of the surroundings (a dissociation reaction). She was brought to a séance led by a medium and put into a trance possession during which she screamed unintelligible words, fainted, and had convulsion-like movements of a sexual nature. After she came out of the trance, an assistant medium went into a trance, adopted the persona of a good spirit, and confronted the girl, warning her that she was not an adult and that dangerous things could happen to her in the streets when she went wandering. The girl was not impressed, whereupon the medium became a bad spirit and told the girl that she could not get rid of him and that he would get her into trouble when she went out on the streets. The girl panicked at this and told the bad spirit to leave her alone. Lubchansky and his colleagues interpreted this as follows. Initially, the medium acted as her superego while she played the role of the observing ego. When this did not produce therapeutic results, the medium acted as her id, and the girl was assaulted by superego anxiety.

This folk therapy of a dissociative reaction involved the therapist switching roles resulting in the girl switching roles along with him. The therapist elicited first the girl's pathological subself and then her healthy subself. The therapy worked – the girl's social adjustment improved, she no longer wandered the streets, and she came regularly to the séances to act out in this safe setting.

Discussion

It is clear that the phenomena discussed in this chapter fall on a continuum of "distancing" or "dissociation." In multiple personality, there is amnesia for the events occurring in other personalities, and amnesia is often present also in possession experiences. In memories of past lives and the spirit controls of mediums, there is no amnesia, but rather the subject locates the experience as coming from an external source (a previous life or the spirit world). The same is true for the auditory hallucinations of schizophrenics which the patient views as coming from "other realms" (Van Dusen, 1973).

In contrast, normal people usually experience their different subselves consciously and acknowledge them as part of the self. They may label these subselves as roles (employee, parent, spouse, etc.), by mood (the depressed self, the happy self, etc.) or in some idiosyncratic way. When they "talk to themselves," they recognize that both "voices" are their own. When they have conflicting desires, they recognize that the opposed desires are all their own.

Interestingly, those who believe in the phenomena described here often use the other phenomena to explain them. Reincarnation phenomena could result from possession (Stevenson & Story, 1970). Multiple personality may be explained as an example of possession (Stevenson, 1977). The auditory hallucinations of schizophrenics are conceived as communications from deceased individuals dwelling in the spirit world (Van Dusen, 1973).

However, the model of the mind as composed of subselves, with varying amounts of dissociation, remains the most parsimonious explanation of all of these phenomena. It explains the phenomena without recourse to explanations (such as reincarnation or a spirit world) which many scientists reject as "unproven," and it does so using a holistic conceptualization of the human mind which has a long history in psychological thought.

The present hypothesis also suggests further research. For example, Ring (1992) studied groups of individuals who reported near-death experiences and alien abductions and found that both groups had a high occurrence of childhood trauma and abuse and high scores on a measure of dissociative tendencies. Lester (2005) found no studies along these lines of those who report reincarnation or possession experiences or on mediums. Such studies would be of great value.

We can, therefore, propose:

POSTULATE 7: Some subselves may be in a dissociated state about which the other selves have delusional, minimal or no knowledge.

COROLLARY 7a: The concept of dissociated subselves can explain such phenomena as multiple personality, possession, mediumship, reincarnation and auditory hallucinations.

The traditional view of dissociated states is that they are pathological. Richards (1990) argued, however, that they may play a major role in growth and transformation. For example, in multiple personality, the client may have a subself (or alter) that is the client as the child who was abused, a persecutor who inflicts pain on the other subselves, and other subselves who represent facets of the personality of the client. The psychotherapist working with such a client may try to identify or create other subselves such a "recorder" who has a memory function and a "helper" who provides guidance and advice. Occasionally, a higher subself can appear or be created who can communicate with the other subselves and who can control which subself takes over (assumes executive control of) the client's mind at any point in time.

Richards discussed whether fusion of the subselves in cases of multiple personality was always the best outcome for the client, or whether co-existence, with good communication and cooperation is preferred. Richards notes that those who become mediums or channelers (Klimo, 1987) can be seen to have chosen (perhaps unconsciously) the latter tactic.

Richards wondered whether each subself can move toward psychological health independently or must the community of subselves move along the path together. Would the techniques of group and family therapy assist the psychotherapist, if the latter tactic was chosen. If one subself is pathological, perhaps isolating that subself would be beneficial for the client. Richards argued that a democratic internal cooperative effort on the part of the subselves was the best tactic, with good communication between the subselves, each of which must be given permission to exist. However, the executive subself must be strengthened once it has been "elected" through internal diplomacy.

Chapter 8

THE CONSTRUCTION AND DESCRIPTION OF THE MULTIPLE SELF

> "You're not taking this seriously," whispered her daemon. "Behave yourself."
> Her daemon's name was Pantalaimon, and he was currently in the form of a moth, a dark brown one so as not to show up in the darkness of the hall.
> "They're making too much noise to hear from the kitchen," Lyra whispered back. "And the Steward doesn't come in till the first bell. Stop fussing."
>
> (Pullman, 1995, p. 3)

Is the multiple self theory of personality proposed in this book a constructivist psychology? Raskin (2002) noted that constructivist psychologies propose that people create ways for meaningfully understanding their worlds and experiences. "Modern" theories were based on empirical research, scientific methodology, and the identification of objective truths, all of which constitutes logical positivism (Sexton, 1997). Sexton noted that, in contrast, "postmodern" theories assume that we create, rather than discover, personal and social realities. Postmodern theories argue that there is no objective view of the world, merely constructed meanings. Raskin noted that constructivist theories fit into this postmodern mold. In the realist (modern) approach, objects exist independently of our sensory and cognitive experience, whereas in the idealist (postmodern) approach, "no material objects or external realities exist apart from our knowledge or consciousness of them (Chiari & Nuzzo, 1996, p. 166).

Raskin (2002) proposed three types of constructivist theories.

1 *Empirical constructivists* accept the existence of an external reality independent of the observer. However, people are aware of this reality only through their constructions of it. Knowledge depends on individual constructions, which are useful fictions for understanding the world. People cannot be sure about the independent reality, but they are aware of whether their constructions of it help them predict the external world.
2 *Hermeneutic constructivists* do not believe in the existence of a reality independent of the observer. Knowledge and understanding are products of individual constructions, influenced largely by language.
3 *Limited realists* accept that external reality exists and that it is possible for people to know it directly. But human perception and understanding is fallible (and, we might add, human information processing is limited), so that people's knowledge of reality is imperfect. Chiari and Nuzzo (1996) noted that cognitive therapists such as Albert Ellis (1962) and Aaron Beck (1976), whose theories are based on the assumption that people often think irrationally (that is, hold irrational or untrue premises), argue that irrational thinking leads people to distort reality.

It is important that psychological theories also make sense to us, that is, fit with our experience. We can make a distinction between external reality and internal reality. External reality is diverse. Material objects, let us say, this book as you read it, are not based to any great extent, if at all, on our construction of it. (Our emotional reaction to it and the desires it arouses, on the other hand, are to a large extent a result of the constructions we place on the book.) People in our external reality also exist, but the constructions we place on other people (human material objects) are much more important to us. Whether we see these particular people as friendly or hostile, for example, determines how we react to them, and the constructions we place on them become of paramount importance.

Internal reality is completely different. Internal reality, an introspective experience, is never observable to others. It is known only to ourselves. There is no way that we can check on this internal reality by asking another person for confirmation. As young people, many of you perhaps wondered whether the sensation you have when you look at a red object, say, is that same sensation as that experienced by others. Do we all "see" red in the same way? It is impossible to know.

Internal reality is also greatly affected by distortions. In many theories of human behavior, distortions play a major role, from the defense mechanisms described by psychoanalytic theory to the irrational thinking described by cognitive therapists. Feedback from our psychotherapists, apparently more objective observers of ourselves, often shocks us. Our love for our parents is really a reaction formation process acting on our hatred of them! Rejection by our lover is not really catastrophic; it is merely inconvenient, and thinking of it as catastrophic is the causal factor for our severe depression and anxiety.

We may debate whether postmodern constructive theories play that great role in our perception of external reality, but it is clear that constructivist theories play an enormous role in our perception of ourselves.

POSTMODERNISM AND THE SELF

Butt, Burr and Bell (1997) noted that modernist psychology assumed that a single, unified self existed. Lay theories of psychology advise, "be true to yourself," "find yourself," and "get in touch with your feelings." This "real self" which underlies our behavior gives us a sense of agency. Butt and his colleagues argued that this concept of a unitary self becomes a form of social control since the individual become self-scrutinizing and self-controlling, thereby making external controls less necessary. Traditional psychotherapy reinforces this oppressive subjectivity. Butt and his colleagues argued that postmodern thought, "offers an opportunity to escape from the tyranny of the unitary self" (p. 16). They see the concept of a multiple self as enabling individuals to see the relational nature of the self, that is, that the "self" differs in each relationship in which the individual engages. They noted that this awareness may result in feelings of inauthenticity, but it is also liberating since now people can "explore and develop different ways of being in different contexts" (p. 16).

Of course, this analysis applies only to subselves that are defined in terms of relationships, subselves such as father, professor, waitress, and so on. The analysis does not applied to subselves that are intrapsychic, such as the depressed self, the mediator or the impulsive self.

PERSONAL CONSTRUCT THEORY[19]

George Kelly (1955) proposed a theory of the structure of the mind based upon cognitive processes (thinking). His basic idea was that we attempt to interpret and make sense of the events that we experience. Our psychological

---

[19] For a more thorough description of Kelly's theory, see Lester (1995).

processes and our behaviors are determined by the way in which we anticipate events (or in Kelly's terms, how we construe events).

At the highest level of abstraction, we can be seen as having a construction system (which is, in effect, a theory of the world). Usually, we seek to extend and refine our construction system. We try to develop a construction system that applies to more and more of the experiences that we encounter, and we try to make it more accurate in the predictions it makes.

Clearly, the theory is a growth-oriented theory in which we become more skilled in making sense of the world in which we live. For Kelly, the model for human behavior is the theoretical scientist who proposes a theory of some phenomenon and then tries to modify the theory to account for all the new data that empirical scientists accumulate about the phenomenon.

As we continue to exist, therefore, we experience more and more, and so our construction system changes and becomes a more accurate predictor for future events. However, it is possible to have inconsistencies and incompatibilities in our construction system. The view of the world we have when we are depressed is often quite different from that which we have when we are happy. When we use only one part of our construction to interpret today's events, we are said to have *suspended* the remaining inconsistent parts.

The Basic Concepts

Construction systems are composed of *constructs*, concepts which we apply to events when we experience them. Constructs are bipolar and dichotomous. When we construe an event we decided that it is *either* this *or* that. Each of us has idiosyncratic constructs. For example, at graduate school, I had a professor who classified people on the basis of their ability as either intelligent versus handicapped. Kelly stressed that it was important to find out how *both* ends of constructs were labelled by people since they may not use the same label as we would. I might use "stupid" as the opposite of intelligent, but my professor used "handicapped."

Types of Constructs

Kelly was not concerned with identifying particular constructs that are commonly used; rather, he defined various properties of constructs. Constructs have a *range of convenience*, a set of events or objects to which they are typically applied. Constructs may be *preverbal* because we developed them before we had good language skills to symbolize them. Constructs may be *propositional*, that is, classification of an event with one construct does not imply anything about how it will be classified in other constructs, or the opposite, *constellatory*. Constellatory thinking is illustrated by sexist and racist ideas. If you meet a man about whom you know nothing and say, "This is a man; therefore he is rational, insensitive, cold, brutal and oppresses women," you are construing in a constellatory manner.

Constructs may be applicable to your conception of your innermost self, in which case they are called *core* constructs; or only tangentially relevant to your sense of self, in which case they are called *peripheral* constructs. In general, psychotherapy deals with your core constructs while education deals with your peripheral constructs.

Construction Systems

Construction systems, or parts of them, may be *tight* or *loose*. In tight construing, your theory of the world makes clear unambiguous predictions about what will happen. In loose construing, your theory does not make clear predictions. Daydreams employ tight thinking in general, while dreams employ loose thinking. Creative thinking is frequently loose but, in order to communicate creative ideas to others, tightening of the ideas must occur. (Einstein's early musing on his innovative ideas in physics might well have passed through a loose period, but to publish the ideas for others to read and use required tightening of them.)

The Perceptual Field

The *perceptual field* is what we experience. It is our subjective perception of the external world. If we explore this external world and seek to gain new experiences, we are said to be *dilating*. On the other hand, if we withdraw from new experiences and retreat into a more well-known world, we are said to be *constricting*.

Reconceptualization of Familiar Concepts

In addition to defining a new set of concepts, Kelly also considered that the traditional meaning of some familiar terms could be improved, in particular by looking at their implications from the person's point of view and from a personal construct perspective. For example, *threat* was redefined as an anticipation that you are about to experience some events that will necessitate a substantial change in your core constructs. This will involve a reconceptualization of who you really are and will involve developing a new set of constructs. We commonly call this an identity crisis.

When you are confronted with evidence that shows that your construction system is incorrect or inadequate in its predictions, you can seek to modify your construction system so that it becomes more adequate. If instead, you seek to distort the evidence so that it remains consistent with your old construction system, you are said to be *hostile*.

The use of psychoanalytic defense mechanism (which involve the distortion of evidence) is a hostile act. Hostility may also involve extorting evidence from the environment that is consistent with your old construction system. Most of the strategies decribed by Festinger (1957) in his theory of cognitive dissonance are hostile. The smoker who, for example, does not notice the warning on the package saying that smoking is hazardous to his health or who refuses to believe that smoking causes lung cancer is behaving in a hostile fashion.

Comment

According to personal construct theory, the self is viewed as constructed rather than discovered – it is the way that individuals construe themselves at each point in time. In particular, the core constructs are critical to people's conception of themselves. Raskin (2002) placed George Kelly's personal construct theory into the category of empirical constructivism, although there is some debate about this. Some constructivists see personal construct theory as too dependent on the existence of an external reality which we must accurately predict for the theory to be a genuine constructivist theory (Chiari & Nuzzo,1996), while some personal construct theorists dislike the theory being viewed as a constructivist theory at all, which they view as a passing fad (Fransella, 1995) and which may distort the theory by casting it as a nothing-but constructivist theory.

THE CONSTRUCTION AND DESCRIPTION OF THE SELF

The theory proposed in the present book has postulated that the mind can usefully be conceptualized as a made up of a set of subselves. On the other hand, Corollary 1a allowed that not everyone may have a plural or multiple self. The mind of some people may usefully be conceptualized as a plural self, but not necessarily the mind of every individual. Alternatively, we can propose that some people construe their minds as a plural self, whereas other people construe their minds as a single self.

If we consider those who construe their minds as plural selves, how might we compare these different subselves? If we are comparing different people, we can, of course, give a structured personality test to each member of the group and compare their scores on the dimensions of personality assessed by the test. When all of the "personalities" are contained in the same person, this becomes less feasible. We would have to "set" the person in one of his or her subselves (or wait until they spontaneously set in one of their subselves), and then administer a personality test while they were in that "set." We would have to do this for each of the subselves he or she reported to us. Sitting down to complete the personality test, might however, change the set that the person was in.

Even if this were possible, what psychological test would be interesting to administer? Given that we are dealing with ordinary people (rather than psychiatric patients or criminals), to find, for example, that one subself was more introverted than another would be of only very limited interest.

One approach resolves these two dilemmas. First, several of the subjects in Lester's (1992) study of subselves described their subselves in terms of roles. For example, one student labeled her subselves as student, mother and counselor. Although not everyone would so label their subselves, our roles typically engender different thoughts, emotions, desires, and behavioral styles from one another. Thus, in some sense, we are different "people" when we are in each of our different roles. Furthermore, as Rowan (1990) and Lester (1992) found, the labelling of subselves differs from person to person, and each of us would find it hard to use the labels proposed by someone else. Roles, however, have a more universal application.

> POSTULATE 8: Kelly's REP Grid technique may be useful for describing and measuring the content of subselves.

For exploring his theory of personality and for use with clients in psychotherapy, Kelly (1955) needed a way of determining which constructs each of us has. He realized that most of us are not used to thinking introspectively about these psychological processes, and so he devised a test, called the Role Construct Repertory Test, or REP Test, to help us identify our constructs. The original REP Test used a grid with 22 columns and 22 rows. At the top of the grid we place our own name and the names of 21 people we have encountered in our lives, ranging from family to supervisors, lovers to friends. Then we take three of these people at a time (determined by circles on the grid) and decide "what do two of them have in common, and how do these two differ from the third?" The words we choose become the two poles of the construct. We then place a checkmark under everyone who has, say, the property represented by the first pole of the construct. We then move to the second row, etcetera, until we have done this twenty-two times.

The completion of Kelly's REP Grid is not an easy task -- it requires a relatively sophisticated person. The present study was conducted on students taking an undergraduate course on Theories of Personality who had already studied Kelly's theory and who had been given a REP Grid to take home to complete for their own self-exploration. They had not, however, been introduced to the notion of subselves.

Since they were students, it was obvious that they all had two roles that they could identify with - student and member of their family, however defined. (Some may have been living at home with parents, while others were old enough to be married, possibly with children.) Therefore, the students were administered a REP Grid to complete as if they were students and as if they were a family member.

This was accomplished by having them place different figures on the two REP Grids. For their role as students, they were asked to place the names of professors at the heads of each column; for their roles as family members, they were asked to place the names of family members at the heads of each column. Thus, each REP Grid required them to sort different types of people.

Since the full 22-by-22 REP Grid was too long (and every student might not know 22 professors and or have 22 family members to place on their REP Grids), they were given two 8-by-8 REP Grids. On the first, they placed the names of eight professors, and on the second they placed the names of eight family members. They were then presented with eight sortings (that is, eight rows with three people highlighted for each row) for each REP Grid. Thus, the students completed two 8-by-8 REP Grids, one for their role as a student and one for their role as a family member.

Of course, the constructs identified are relevant only to the individual taking the REP Grid. Kelly himself proposed no postulates or corollaries concerned with the particular words used for the constructs and their contrasts (that is, the two poles of the construct). However, later researchers have measured the cognitive complexity of the responses to the REP Grids, and the present study subjected each of the REP Grids completed by the students to a factor analysis of constructs to identify how many factors could be identified and what percentage of the variance was accounted for by the first (major) factor.

Secondly, each student was asked to list the eight constructs identified for professors and the eight constructs identified for family members and then rate each on a scale from 1 to 7 for how appropriate each construct was for describing each of their professors and each of their family members. This enabled a test of the hypothesis that the constructs identified for professors would be viewed as more appropriate for describing professors than for describing family members, and vice versa for the constructs identified for describing family members. Responses were obtained from 25 students with a mean age of 25.1 years (standard deviation 6.9); twenty were women and five were men.

How complex were the REP Grid responses produced by the students? The REP Grid responses were factor analyzed using SPSSX, with a principal components extraction and a varimax rotation. The mean number of factors for the REP Grids for professors was 2.65 (SD = 0.49) and for family members 2.83 (SD= 0.39), a difference which was not statistically significant (t_{22} = 1.28).[20] However, the percentage of variance accounted for the first (major) factor was greater for the REP Grid responses for the professors than for the family members (49.3% versus 41.7%, SDs = 1.03 and 0.77; t_{22} = 3.10, two-tailed p < .01). This indicates that the REP Grid responses for the professors were less complex than those for family members.

When asked about the appropriateness of the two sets of constructs for each group of figures, the constructs identified for professors were rated as more appropriate for professors than for family members (means scores[21] for the eight constructs 19.84 versus 28.42, SDs = 7.67 and 6.69; t_{18} = 4.25, p < .001), whereas the constructs identified for family members were rated as less appropriate for professors than for family members (means 29.47 and 19.47, SDs = 7.80 and 6.56; t_{18} = 4.46, P < .001).

Thus, both hypotheses were supported. The REP Grid responses for professors were less complex on one measure of complexity, and the constructs identified on the two grids were described as more appropriate for the people for whom they were identified than for the other group.

---

[20] Some subjects had missing data.
[21] A low score means more appopriate.

Putting this in a less technical manner, the theories of interpersonal behavior (construction systems in Kelly's terms) we have developed for family members are more complex than those we have developed for professors, and the theories of interpersonal behavior are better suited for the subselves in which they operate than for other subselves.

Let us look at a specific example. Figure 1 shows the REP Grids completed by a 26 year-old female student for her professors and for her family. (The "circles" in the three cells in each row of the grids are omitted.) The factor analysis for her professors indicated three factors: (1) outspoken and confident, (2) clear, hyper and outgoing, and (3) sensitive, repetitive and lenient. These accounted for 40.0%, 24.8% and 20.4% of the variance respectively.

The responses on her family REP Grid also produced three factors: (1) creative, smart, practical and reserved, (2) affectionate and sensitive, and (3) creative, outspoken and confident. These accounted for 33.1%, 28.3% and 22.3% of the variance respectively. Thus, the first factor for professors accounted for more variance than the first factor for families.

The constructs for professors were rated as more appropriate for professors than for family (scores of 15 versus 22); the constructs for families were rated as more appropriate for families than for professors (scores of 8 versus 32).[22]

Other Methods for Describing Subselves

Other methods may be developed for having individuals describe their subselves. For example, Platman, et al. (1969) had manic-depressive patients describe their emotions while in a manic state, a depressed state and in a normal state using the Profile of Mood States (McNair, et al., 1971). They found that the patients described themselves very differently in the manic and in the depressed states. For example, when in the manic state, the patients reported high levels of acceptance, surprise and joy, and when in the depressed state high levels of sadness, disgust, and anger.

Interestingly, when in a normal state, they viewed their manic emotional state very differently from the way in which they viewed the manic state when manic. In contrast, their description of the depressed state was similar during and after the depressed state. Staff members also rated the emotions shown by the patients in the two states, and their ratings agreed with those of the patients' recall of their

---

[22] On a scale of 1 (very appropriate) to 7 (not appropriate at all), these average out to 1.87 versus 2.75 and 1.00 versus 4.00 when divided by 8 (for the number of constructs in each set)

emotional states. This suggested that patients, when manic, have an incorrect perception of their emotional state, but not when depressed.

Butt and his colleagues (1997) asked eleven people to choose eight or nine others with whom they had relationships. They were presented with the names of two at a time and asked to consider similarities and difference in how they experienced themselves in the relationships. The result was a list of constructs for each person. They then completed a more formal Grid in which the eight or nine people were the column anchors.

Butt and his colleagues found that their subjects articulated the varied ways in which they experienced themselves and behaved in the different relationships. They felt themselves to be quite different people in the different relationships. For example, "Ken" felt that he could his real self in only two of his relationship – those with his father and with "Clare." Yet he also acknowledged that he construed himself to be very different in the two relationships – deferential, patient and protected with his father, and impatient, dominating and protective with Clare. Thus, Ken was "himself" in both relationships, but very different in each. Butt and his colleagues noticed that their subjects felt themselves to be their real selves when they did not have to self-conscious and on guard. They could be spontaneous and at ease.

All of the subjects recognized that they produced different selves in different social situations. These different selves were not arranged in any hierarchical manner, but rather were grouped somewhat anarchistically, with each self having a similar status. Burr and his colleagues concluded that, "[t]he postmodern subject recognizes its own diversity" (p. 26).

COMMENT

The aim of the present chapter was to illustrate how we might describe subselves in an abstract way so that the many subselves of each person may be compared and the subselves of different people may be compared, and second how we might derive testable hypotheses about subselves.

The research demonstrated that George Kelly's constructivist theory of personality and measurement techniques are useful for describing and measuring the content of subselves. In particular, the research has suggested that each subself may be ideally suited for the role it has and be less useful if applied in other roles. Kelly's theory discusses the possibility that alternative, possibly inconsistent construction systems may exist side-by-side, and he suggested that, when one is operating (that is, has control of the mind), then the others are "suspended." This process may be necessary to prevent inappropriate selves operating in situations.

Secondly, it was argued in this chapter that the multiple self theory of personality is a postmodern and constructivist theory in that it permits individuals to describe their mind in their own unique and idiosyncratic way. The theory imposes fewer constraints than most theories of personality. Indeed, it even permits individuals to reject the theory (Corollary 1a)!

    Your age: ____years
    Your Gender: ____male   ____female

On the REP Grid below, write the names of eight professors you know best in the spaces at the head of the eight columns. You can use their names, first names or initials (or a code if you do not want me to see their real names). Then, as in the REP Grid, consider the three professors indicated by the three circles in the first row. What do two of them have in common and how do they differ from the third? Write the terms under the construct and contrast. Then check each of the eight professors who possess the quality under the construct. Then go through the same procedure on row two, row three etc. for all eight rows.

The Construction and Description of the Multiple Self 133

							CONSTRUCT	CONTRAST
x	x		x	x		x	LENIENT	STRICT
			x	x			REPETITIVE	NON-REPETITIVE
x	x	x		x	x		OUTGOING	QUIET
x	x	x		x	x		HYPER	RELAXED
x	x	x	x	x	x	x	CLEAR	CONFUSING
x	x	x	x	x	x		x	CONFIDENT	SHY-LACKING CONFIDENCE
x	x	x	x	x	x		x	OUTSPOKEN	SOFTSPOKEN
x	x		x	x	x	x	SENSITIVE	INSENSITIVE

Now, put the names of the eight family members in your family to whom you feel closest in the spaces at the head of each column. Go through the same procedure as in other REP Grids to identify eight constructs and contrasts, and check each person for whether they have the qualities written under the construct.

							CONSTRUCT	CONTRAST
X	x		x	x		x	x	OPEN	RESERVED
x		x		x	x	x	x	PRACTICAL	NOT VERY PRACTICAL
x	x	x	x		x	x	x	CONFIDENT	SHY
x	x		x		x	x	x	OUTSPOKEN	SOFTSPOKEN
x	x	x		x	x	x	x	SMART	NOT ALWAYS WITH IT
x	x	x	x	x	x		x	SENSITIVE	INSENSITIVE
x	x	x	x	x	x		x	AFFECTIONATE	DOESN'T SHOW AFFECTION
x	x	x		x	x	x	CREATIVE	TIGHT THINKER

Figure 8.1: Describing the multiple self

Chapter 9

DEVELOPMENTAL CONSIDERATIONS

I have to live with both my selves as best I may

(Brigitte Bardot, www.celebrina.com/brigitte-bardot/quotes)

The standard developmental path in systems theory is that, "…..it proceeds from a state of relative globality and lack of differentiation to a state of increasing differentiation, articulation, and hierarchic integration" (Werner, 1957, p. 126). This results in an increasing number of relatively autonomous units and increasing integration between these units which implies an increasing number of interrelationships between the units.

ASSIMILATION AND ACCOMMODATION

Following Piaget (Flavell, 1963), it can be proposed that, as the individual encounters more situations and has more accompanying experiences, information is received and, where possible, assimilated (which involves no change in the cognitive structures) and the individual's cognitive structures accommodate (a process whereby the individual's cognitive structure is modified as a result of the individual's experience). Some accommodation is good, but accommodation implies being influenced by others in structuring our experiences (Mehrabian, 1968), and Mehrabian suggested that excessive accommodation may result in the looseness of associations observed in some schizophrenic patients. This looseness of associations may be a result of the schizophrenic responding to disconnected stimulation in the environment.

One extreme form of accommodation behavior is imitation. Individuals, from an early age, imitate those around them, including significant others, teachers, peers, and even characters in books, movies and video games and on television. Not only do humans imitate the behaviors of others, but they also imitate the thinking style and patterns, as well as specific attitudes and values of others. In psychoanalytic theory, this process is called identification. Some subselves may form by this process of imitation or identification.

A Critical Issue

A critical issue here is how many levels there may be in an individual between the system as a whole and the individual psychological forces (thoughts, emotions, desires and behaviors). Are there only subsystems, or can there be subsubsystems, subsubsubsystems, and so on? A simple proposal for development is that the number of levels increases as the individual matures and the number of units within each level also increases. Perhaps we can propose that there are a finite number of levels and a finite number of units within each level. However, the multiple self theory of the mind proposed in this book has assumed only one level, that of subselves. It is possible to add additional levels (and talk of subsubselves, for example), but we have not done so here.

Deverlopmental Postulates and Corollaries

A simple postulate that covers developmental aspects of subselves is

POSTULATE 9: The set of subselves that constitute the mind of an individual changes with age

The question, therefore, is what are the processes that govern these changes. How do new subselves develop and what is their source? There are several mechanisms by which new subselves can be created.

Introjected Subselves

COROLLARY 9a: There are subselves formed by the introjection of the desires and thoughts of powerful others (in particular, parental figures) and imitation of their personality and behavioral styles

In Chapter 3 where the existence of subselves common to all people was addressed, the concept of the façade self was introduced, and it was proposed that almost every individual has a façade self. Angyal's pattern of vicarious living, one half of his bionegative system principle, argued that this subself developed because, to use Carl Roger's terminology, parents impose conditions of worth on the child so that the child, in order to gain its parents' approval and love, suppresses the real self and adopts a façade self of which the parents approve.

COROLLARY 9b: Subselves may be formed as a result of early experiences.

Subselves Formed as a Result of Threat

Threat was defined by George Kelly in his theory of personal constructs in a way quite differently from that found in dictionaries. Kelly defined threat as an awareness that a comprehensive change was imminent in your core constructs, that is, in your conception of yourself. In the broadest sense, threat can be induced when we perceive any plausible alternative to our core constructs.

For me, I often feel threat whenever I meet anyone who leads a different life style from mine. My initial thought is often, "I ought to do that," although on reflection I realize that their choices are not for me. I have colleagues who earn extra money by consulting and some who do so by being psychotherapists. Ought I to do that too? No! I once had a colleague who had a wife and two children, two mistresses whose rents he paid, and several girlfriends; he had two full-time jobs and four part-time jobs. I had one wife, one child, no mistresses, and only one job. He led me to think that I was not making good use of my time! I have a colleague at my college who makes me feel like a dilettante. We both started akido together. He is now a black belt; I dropped out after a semester. I barely keep plants alive; he grows prize-winning orchids. I take photographs on my travels for my albums; he has exhibitions of his photographs. And so on. I explained Kelly's notion of threat to him one day as he was giving me a shiatzu massage. Of course, he has never written a book. Maybe I'm a threat to him?

In contrast to threat, Kelly defined fear as an awareness that a minor change is imminent in your core constructs, and this is a much less interesting state of mind. In Kelly's theory, it should be noted that we do not consciously and purposely seek out threat and fear. Typically, these states are generated in us by situations and peole we encounter in the course of our life.

Threat, therefore, in Kelly's definition means that other people can embody selves that we can consider as additions to our set of subselves. We do not have to adopt them exactly as lived by others, but they are often enticing, and we can model a new subself on the life style that they demonstrate.

COROLLARY 9c: Subselves may be formed by the encountering of possible subselves exemplified by other people.

Regressive Subselves

COROLLARY 9d: There are probably regressive subselves in most, if not all, individuals which are the subselves that they had at an earlier stage in life.

The clearest proposal of regressive subselves comes from Eric Berne's Transactional Analysis (see Chapters 1 and 6) in his analysis of ego states. In his structural analysis, Berne classified the psychological processes of the person into three parts.

Parent -- identifying ego state
Adult -- data processing ego state
Child -- regressive ego state

In Chapter 1, it was noted that the Parent ego state is a judgmental ego state, but in an imitative way (primarily, of course, by imitating the person's parental judgments). It seeks to enforce borrowed standards. The Adult ego state is concerned with transforming stimuli into information and processing that information. The Child ego state reacts impulsively, using prelogical thinking and poorly differentiated and distorted perception.

The analysis of ego states can be made much more complex. A small child has three ego states: a Parent ego state, and Adult ego state, and a Child ego state. When a trauma occurs that fixes these ego states, all three are fixed. As a result, a particular Child ego state that an adult has, in fact, has three components: a primitive Child ego state, a primitive Adult ego state, and a primitive Parent ego state. Similarly, this primitive Child can be subdivided into three ego states (Parent, Adult and Child), and so on. The Child ego state of an adult has, therefore, many components.

The Parent ego state is an introjection of our parents' demands. But we had two parents. Therefore, our Parent ego state is a dual ego state. Secondly, our parents had three ego states, and they also had parents (our grandparents) and so on.

An issue that Berne did not address is whether there can be several ego states that are Adult, or Child, or Parent? Transactional analysts talk as if there are only three ego states – one Parent, one Adult and one Child – although they allow each ego state to have several components. There is no reason for this assumption. If we free ourselves from the boundaries set by transactional analysis, then we can propose the existence of more than one regressive (Child) ego state (and, in addition, more than one introjected [Parent] ego state).

We can see, therefore, that regressive subselves can exist, that is, subselves that we once possessed and which are childlike, and which can reappear later in life and assume executive power over the mind.

Future Subselves

COROLLARY 9e: Individuals can seek to create new subselves for the future

There is a distinction that can be made between the *façade self* and the *ideal self*. Both of these subselves are derived from demands that parents and others impose upon children. The façade self, however, is the subself that controls the mind when we interact with others. The ideal self, in contrast, embodies a way that we would like to be if we could achieve that state but which we probably will never achieve. For example, when I lecture to my college classes, my mind and behavior is controlled by one of my façade selves, but there is also an ideal self that I imagine, a subself that I will never achieve. It has components such as achieving Zen Buddhist sartori, never being driven by my unfulfilled desires, never getting angry, and many other aspirations. The ideal self is, therefore, a *possible self*, to use a concept proposed by (Markus and Nurius (1986).

Markus and Nurius suggested that "possible selves derive from representations of the self in the past and they include representations of the self in the future" (p. 954). They are imagined roles or states of being and represent our hopes, fears and fantasies. Although possible selves are not subselves (since possible selves are not organized systems of psychological elements), they may derive from introjected desired and so resemble ideal selves and may be goals toward which individuals aspire.

THE IMPACT OF AGING

COROLLARY 9f: Individuals form fewer possible selves as they age. Aging narrows the possibilities for the individual as he or she moves toward completing their specific system principle.

According to Angyal's theory of personality, we develop our personal version of the general system principle (the trends toward autonomy and homonomy), or in Berne's Transactional Analysis our specific, unique script (Steiner, 1974). Thereafter, the course of life is the progressive realization of this idiosyncratic system principle. As we age, there are fewer and fewer options, because the particular version of the system principle that the individual has chosen must be completed. In this sense, therefore, we become more rigid as we grow older for it is too late to choose an alternative specific system principle to guide our lives.

It is interesting how common it is for people to die once they complete their specific system principle. Abraham Maslow, a few years before his retirement and death, told me that he had laid out a scholarly path for himself some 30 years earlier. He had wanted to accomplish particular goals and to explore particular topics from the humanistic perspective that he had developed. At the time we talked, he told me that he was working on the final paper he had planned those many years ago. He completed it, retired, and died soon after, a not uncommon occurrence (Weisman and Hackett, 1961; Lester, 1970). In his role as scholar, he had fashioned a particular form for his system principle, and he had wanted and needed to complete the plan, which he accomplished.

SELECTING AND REJECTING SUBSELVES

Perhaps with the help of a psychotherapist, we can identify, examine and make judgments about our subselves. Are all of them appropriate for us at the stage of development we find ourselves? Should some be retired? Should others be developed? This leads to a new corollary.

COROLLARY 9g: Subselves are selected to become more or less permanent members of the plural self depending on their usefulness in helping the individual succeed.

INTEGRATION

If the mind is conceptualized as made up of several subselves, the issue arises as to how the mind might be integrated (Lester, 1987). Several theories of personality state that the psychologically healthy person is integrated, including the theories proposed by Carl Jung and Fritz Perls, although integration is typically seen as a task of the second half of life (for example, in the theories of Erik Erikson and Carl Jung). We spend the first half of our lives exploring our selves, identifying our desires and interests, which often are in conflict and, later, we integrate these. What then does the term integration mean? Lester (1987) reviewed several ways in which the term is used.

In Angyal's theory of personality, we have two competing system principles, and each system principle has two component parts. Angyal's theory suggests two solutions. First, Angyal proposed the existence of two competing organizations of the mind: a healthy organization which he called biopositive and an unhealthy organization which he called bionegative. He proposed that the mind is always organized by one or by the other. As the person becomes more psychologically healthy, the biopositive organization controls the mind for longer and longer period. Complete health would mean that the bionegative organization never assumes control of the mind. Thus, the goal for the healthy person is for the unhealthy system principle to be deprived of any executive power. One system principle eliminates the other.

Second, the healthy system principle has two components, the trends toward autonomy and homonomy, and the goal is for these two parts to peacefully coexist in the healthy (or eupsychian) mind. One trend does not eliminate the other. They must combine so that each behavior is, in part, an expression of both trends.

In Freud's psychoanalytic theory, for example, the goal of psychoanalysis is to move unconscious thoughts, desires, and emotions into consciousness. Thus, all of the psychological materials will move from being in two subsystems (the conscious and the unconscious) to being in one single system, and none of the content is lost. This parallels Angyal's second solution above.

Vargiu (1974) described several forms of integration, including time-sharing (where each subself has control of the mind on some occasions), cooperation, absorption (where one subself absorbs another), fusion or merging, and finally synthesis, which Vargiu sees as a transpersonal movement.

At the subself level of analysis, these examples suggest three possibilities.

1. It could be that, toward the end of life, all but one of the subselves are eliminated, leaving one single subself in existence in the mind, thereby achieving integration.
2. It may be that the contents of all of the subselves are fused into one subsystem, and the contents reorganized to form a unified single self.
3. It may be that the subselves live together in peaceful harmony, functioning as a friendly, cooperating group, coexisting in harmony with one another as Shapiro and Elliott (1976) suggested. Some theories see the subsystems as having impermeable boundaries, and combination of the different subsystems into one single whole would be a mistake. For example, it would not necessarily be a good idea to combine my different roles (as teacher, husband, son, father, scholarly colleague, and friend) all into one single role. There is merit in maintaining the roles separate. Integration in this perspective would be harmony between the various subsystems, much like a smoothly functioning group of people or family. Similarly, in Berne's Transactional Analysis, the goal is to have each ego state develop a firm, impermeable boundary so that other ego states cannot intrude into (or contaminate) one another. These three ego states then coexist in harmony.

These considerations lead to one postulate and five corollaries.

POSTULATE 10: The individual eventually tries to integrate the subselves.

COROLLARY 10a: The integration of subselves is a task for the second half of life.
COROLLARY 10b: One form of integration is the elimination of all subselves but one.
COROLLARY 10c: One form of integration is the fusion or merging of the separate subselves into a single unified self.
COROLLARY 10d: One form of integration is peaceful and harmonious coexistence, cooperation and collaboration between the subselves.
COROLLARY 10e: It is a clinical issue as to which individuals choose each path of integration and what determines this choice.

Corollaries 10b and 10c result in the individual having a single self. For those theorists who prefer to believe in a single self, at least at some stage of development and maturity, then selfhood is easily seen as rooted in this single self. Corollary 10d, in which several subselves coexist in peaceful harmony, implies that selfhood is a more dynamic concept. Selfhood is whatever subself has executive control at the time. When I am happy, then my sense of self is defined by that subself. When, a few days later, I am depressed, then my sense of self changes to be defined by the new subself.

THE CONTENT OF SUBSELVES

Although the multiple self theory of the mind proposes no common content shared by all individuals, the content of subselves formed at different ages could be influenced by the stage that the individual is in, for example, the psychoanalytic oral, anal and phallic stages, or Erikson's (1959) eight stages from "trust versus mistrust" through to "integrity versus despair." The content may move from egocentric to relational. Early subselves may be bound by sensorimotor input and perceptual input (preverbal and unconscious), whereas later subselves may be more abstract (explicit and conscious).

As we move from sensorimotor to perceptual to cognitive functioning, each stage of development involves more differentiation and more hierarchical organization and an increasing differentiation of the self from the environment (Mehrabian, 1968). Mehrabian, in his discussion of cognitive development, proposed that the existence of many subordinate and less abstract cognitions (here we can substitute the term subselves), the easier it is to develop superordinate or abstract cognitions since development involves increasing differentiation and integration of existing cognitions.

Chapter 10

APPLICATIONS OF SUBSELF THEORY

You talk to yourself. You're not unique at that. Every one of us does that. We carry on internal talk.....In fact we maintain our world with our internal talk. (Carlos Castaneda, 1972, p. 218-219)

The concept of subselves is common in discussions of human behavior, although the discussions are not usually phrased in this way. This chapter will examine some discussions of behavior that fit into the notion of subselves.

SHIFTING

Jones and Shorter-Gooden (2003) have discussed the particular problems that black professional women face as a result of both sexism and racism in our society. To cope with this, black women do what Jones and Shorter-Gooden call *shifting*. They "change the way that they think of things or the expectations that they have for themselves. Or they alter their outward appearance. They modify their speech. They shift in one direction at work each morning, then in another at home each night" (p. 61).

Jones and Short-Gooden admit, of course, that all of us do this to some extent, whatever our sex or ethnicity. Our role (or subself) at work is often different from our role (or subself) at home, but the shifting is much greater for black professional women because of the ways in which blacks and women are perceived in the workplace. What is especially difficult for black professional women is that, if they do not shift back in the evening when they are home, then they are accused of becoming too "white" by their African-American friends and relatives. As one woman interviewed put it: "I have to gotta go home and wash some of the White off me" (p. 77). If I maintain my "professorial" demeanor outside of my college, I never get admonished for it. Quite the opposite – I am usually told how well I am dressed and how handsome I have become. Black professional women, on the other hand, may be expected to change their clothes, their speech patterns and their demeanor to fit in with a relaxed African American cultural style. Similarly, dreadlocks and African robes do not make their role easier in managerial meetings at work.

Shifting can secure survival in the two worlds, but it can also be self-destructive. On the positive side, it can allow the individual to explore different and genuine parts of herself, to connect with a wide variety of people and to explore opportunities. On the other hand, it can lead them to lose touch with their inner, authentic experience as they create the façade that they need for work. As "she acquiesces to the tyranny of their biases, needs, and expectation, [s]he feels frustrated, lonely, and inadequate" (p. 64).

When they are at work, the women continually have to scan, survey and scrutinize the environment, deciding how to respond. They have to suppress and block the feelings of sadness, anger, disappointment, anxiety and shame. They seeking spiritual and emotional support if they are able, and often retreat to the black community and abide by the "home" codes (which are often also sexist!).

TEACHING PERSONAE

Showalter (2003), in writing about teaching, noted that all teachers develop a persona, a façade self, which we adopt when we teach. This persona may be an exaggeration of our private self or an evasion of it. Showalter noted a gender difference here, with female teachers adopting more often a self-effacing or self-deprecating persona, while male teachers more often adopt authoritative or eccentric roles. For example, she noted that J. R. R. Tolkien, an Oxford University instructor and the author of *The Lord of the Rings*, usually wore a tweed jacket and smoked a pipe, the traditional image of an Oxbridge don, sometimes walked silently to the podium in the lecture hall and then burst into the opening lines of Beowulf, shouting them in the original Anglo-Saxon.

As teachers age, their personae change too. What fitted us when we were close in age to the students is no longer quite appropriate when they are the age of our children (and then grandchildren). Our students no longer share our world view, and the examples we bring from life often took place decades before they were born. Even the step of obtaining tenure can have an impact on our persona since our anxiety about job security (and avoiding any negative feedback from the students) is less of a concern. Obtaining a full professorship can have a similar impact since, at that point, we have achieved all that we can at the institution.

Showalter felt that it was important to fit the persona to the content of one's lecture and scholarship. Some teachers, however, never give their persona any critical appraisal and may have a classroom presence that is less impressive and less coherent than their writing. Showalter described one Harvard University professor (Reuben Brower) who spoke in a high-pitched, monotonous voice, answered questions before the student had finished asking them (thereby often misunderstanding the question), and often asked for a few more minutes when the class period was over despite the fact that students were closing their notebooks and leaving. In contrast, as a literary critic, he preferred short tight forms such as lyric poetry. He liked closure in his writing but resisted this in his teaching.

Showalter argued that "anti-establishment Marxists" should not be authoritarian and rigid; "feminist" scholars should learn how to handle the classroom equipment, and "hippies" should not be sticklers about deadlines. Showalter, therefore, argues for consistency between the teacher's different personae, that the teaching persona should match the scholarly persona and also be consistent with one's intellectual views.

Students note the teacher's persona and try to "psych out" the teacher based on it. The teaching style, as well as sartorial choices, are important pieces of information to supplement the course syllabus and help the students gauge what they need to do to get their preferred grade in the course.

Parini (2005) waxed more lyrically about teaching personae. Parini views each Fall as an opportunity to try on a new persona:

> .....those brittle masks we mold to our skin, that eventually become indistinguishable from what we call the self, that many-faceted figurations we present to the world. (p. 3)

Parini noted that transitions are good opportunities to switch masks – when switching from one school to another, going off to college, becoming a professor and, thereafter, each new academic year.

Parini views the classroom as a form of theater in which the professors play various roles (both as actor and as dramatist), roles that are often exaggerated. Parini listed wise man, fool, tempter, comforter, coach and confessor (p. 6). "Authenticity" is a fiction. What is interesting here is that Parini acted in plays in high school, quite successfully, and he sees his acting skills and theater experience as laying the foundation for his teaching self. It would be interesting to study the subselves of actors, both in terms of whether they find the concept appropriate, the number of subselves they can list, and the way in which they describe these subselves.

At the beginning of his professorial career, Parini found it hard to find a teaching self, and he noted that, without a clear teaching self, he felt disconnected from his classes and inadequate as a teacher. He noted that, at times, he drew on models – teachers he had in school and university – and modeled his classes on them. Even as he draws near to retirement, Parini is "still working to create a face, or faces, that will prove useful, true, and distinct. My magic closet is now full of masks; some fit well, others don't" (p. 69).

One thing that is of interest in both Showalter's and Parini's discourses on teaching selves is that both of them gave the concept conscious thought - Parini especially as his own career progressed. Parini described a colleague who practiced his lectures at home in front of a mirror. Although, clearly, some professors develop a teaching self in this way, for others, like myself, it develops without conscious thought or planning. As I grew comfortable in the classroom, I "discovered" that I preferred lecturing to leading seminars. I lectured to diverse audiences – initially female students, then coed classes, police officers, groups of employees and, of course, the audiences at various conferences – and again "discovered" that I had a specific teaching self which fitted me well. Parini describes those like me as "lucky." He advises other teachers to work on their teaching self consciously.

DOUBLE LIVES

Heenan (2002) argued that, in order to have a fulfilling life, it is often useful to develop a second passion or vocation (or a second life). In his book, Heenan profiled ten individuals who illustrate this. For example, Winston Churchill was not only a politician who led Great Britain and the Allies to victory over Germany in the Second World War, he was also a painter (and, we might add, an author). His writing provided him with fame and fortune, but painting was his solace, a release from the pressures of governing his country.

In 1915, when he was 41 years old, he watched his sister-in-law painting watercolors, and he decided to try it himself. He says of his hobby, "Painting came to my rescue in a most trying time. I had great anxieties and no means of relieving it. The Muse of Painting came to my rescue" (Heenan, 2002, p. 35).

During the First World War, he was assigned to Belgium in 1915 as a colonel. His junior officers were amazed to see him set up his painting equipment in the midst of battle. For most of the Second World War, he put his painting aside, but in 1943, after a conference with President Franklin Roosevelt in Morocco, he traveled 150 miles inland to paint the snowcapped Atlas Mountains.

In many ways, the "second life" is very different from the major occupation, and the person behaves differently when in this second life. Churchill, a fiery orator and a dynamic and effective ruler, became focused and quiescent when painting. It is as if a subself develops and takes over during this double life.

Perlmutter (2008) urged non-tenured faculty to develop this second life as a way of lessening the anxieties associated with getting tenure, but Heenan urged all of us to develop a second life and gave guidelines for achieving this.

THE PUZZLE OF SELF-REGULATION

The phenomenon of self-deception in which we deceive ourselves, has puzzled some scholars. Deception appears to involve two selves – the deceiver and the deceived - but in self-deception, these two selves are in the same mind (Pears, 1985). One self appears to ignore the truth perceived by the other self. Pears did not think that these two selves should be identified with the conscious and the unconscious mind, but rather suggested that the usefulness of the concept of *functional isolation* in which the subject-self contains elements that do not interact with all of the object-self's elements. The two systems can be conceptualized as overlapping circles. The desire to avoid accepting what the requirement of the total evidence counsels causes this functional isolation.

Schelling (1978) provided similar examples, such as the subself that wants clean lungs and a long life and the other subself who adores tobacco, in which the "irrational" subself discounts the future. This dichotomy is also found in Zen Buddhism. For example, in Zazen, sitting meditation, one subself tries to control another subself. You (one subself) must empty your mind (another subself) of all intrusive thoughts (Watts, 1961).

Self-regulation refers to situations in which people use volition or will in order to set goals and pursue them using intrapsychic processes or by manipulating the environment. For example, it may be that people have to wait some time before they get what they want (delay of gratification). One way to deal with this situation is to distract oneself, focus one's attention on some other activity or thought. A person, waiting in the waiting room of a doctor's office for the news of the outcome of a medical test, can bring along a favorite magazine to read or a sudoku puzzle to solve. To personalize this, in this situation, "I" distract "myself," raising the puzzle of whether the "I" and the "myself" refer to the same entity, for it certainly sounds as if there are two subselves involved.

The ability to self-regulate is often hindered by intrusive thoughts.[23] The desire to give up smoking can be hindered by thoughts such as, "I have no willpower; I cannot do this." Advice on improving performance by means of self-regulation have proposed such strategies as "How to talk to yourself better: Changing internal monologues" (Mischel, 1993), a tactic proposed also by Meichenbaum and Cameron (1974) who have used the term "inner dialogue" (Meichenbaum, 1977, p. 12), thereby implying at least two subsleves. Mechenbaum and Cameron worked with impulsive children, schizophrenics and patients with anxiety disorders, training them to "instruct themselves" when they were involved in particular tasks.[24] Meichenbaum and Cameron modeled this. For example, for the impulsive child, the modeled verbalization was something like the following:

> Okay, what is it I have to do? You want me to copy the picture with the different lines. I have to go slowly and carefully. Okay, draw the line down, down, good; then to the right; that's it; now down some more and to the left. Good. I'm doing fine so far. Remember, go slowly. Now back up again. No, I was supposed to go down. That's okay. Just erase the line carefully.....Good. Even if I make an error I can go on slowly and carefully. Okay, I have to go down now. Finished. I did it! (p. 266)

In this process, individuals are talking to themselves. One subself is addressing another subself. Indeed, Shaffer (1947) defined psychotherapy as a "learning process through which a person acquires an ability to speak to himself in appropriate ways so as to control his own conduct" (p. 463).

Kazdin and Wilson (1978) listed a number of other tactics, including self-observation (carefully monitoring one's own behavior), self-rewarding (congratulating oneself for achieving predetermined goals), self-contracting (for example, promising oneself a tasty snack after one has completed a task), and self-instruction (talking to oneself). It is evident that these tactics resemble the tasks that Shapiro and Elliott (1976) set for their psychotherapy clients when they encourage them to form specific new subselves, such as a "recording secretary," "mediator," and "chairman of the board."

---

[23] See also the section on voice therapy in Chapter 6.
[24] Meichenbaum (1985) also used this technique for stress inoculation training.

Many psychologists also acknowledge that the self has the capacity to be conscious of itself (Mischel, 1993), that is, make oneself the object of one's attention. One subself observes the other subself.

PRESERVING THE RATIONALITY OF HOMO ECONOMICUS

Related to the above is the problem that classical economics faces with its basic assumption that people behavior rationally in their economic behavior. Thaler and Shefrin (1981) noted that, for many years, banks ran Christmas Clubs for which people paid in money regularly to a special account that paid no interest and which they could withdraw only after December 1st. This makes no rational sense since they could easily have paid the same money into a regular bank savings account that paid interest. As Stigler (1966) noted, Christmas Clubs enabled people to protect themselves against a future lack of will power.

Thaler and Shefrin noted that an explanation of this behavior could be based on the concept of a two-self economic man. People have two sets of preferences which can in conflict at a single point in time – short-term and long-term preferences – which Thaler and Shefrin labelled as the "doer" and the "planner." The planner is concerned with lifetime utility, while the doer exists only for one period and is completely selfish, or myopic. (p. 394)

Self-control involves altering the doer's incentives and altering the opportunities. Incentives can be altered by modifying the doer's preferences. People can be persuaded that saving is a good thing to do. Monitoring the behavior is a second strategy, since keeping track acts like a tax on the deviant behavior (not saving). Thirdly, incentives can be explicitly altered, as when a scholar agrees to give a paper at a conference in the future to provide an incentive to write it now.

Opportunities can be altered by such tactics as precommitment (such as paying to go to a "fat farm" which is basically a resort that promises not to feed you) and limiting the range of short-term discretion (such as not allowing people to withdraw money from their Christmas Club account before December 1st). Thaler and Shefrin predicted that people will choose rationally to impose constraints on their own behavior, especially if the benefits and costs incurred by the behavior occur at different times.

Lynne (2006) proposed a modification of the classic economic conceptualization of humans as completely rational by noting that egoistic self-interest which underlies economists' conception of humans is counterbalanced by an empathic other-interest. He called his theory "metaeconomics." There are,

Lynne argued, two competing forces motivating human behavior, and he recognized the similarity of these two forces that he proposed to Andras Angyal's trends toward autonomy and homonomy. Following Angyal's holistic approach to the mind, Lynne preferred to see the two competing forces (self-interest and other-interest) as forming two subselves, and Lynne noted that the dynamic, in which these two subselves achieve a "peace of mind," was similar to Herbert Simon's (1977) process of "satisficing." Lynne noted that classical economics is simply the default case where the other-interest force is zero. Lynne suggested that the conflict (between conflicting forces) has to be conscious for it to be resolved in a rational way. "...[R]ational resolution first requires making the feelings explicit and subjecting them to ration thought and consideration" (p. 105).

Other economists have taken up this notion of two contemporaneous subselves, and they have even identified the planner and the doer with such as constructs as the ego and the id and as the prefrontal cortex and the limbic system in the brain (Bénabou & Pycia, 2002).

DEALING WITH TRAUMATIC SITUATIONS

Occasionally people find themselves in traumatic situations, and in this section we will consider two such situations and explore how the multiple self theory of the mind (in other scholars' hands and under a different label) has been used to explain the response of those traumatized.

The Self When Faced with War

Laufer (1988) explored the impact on young men who have led ordinary lives when sent off to fight in wars. Engaging in war requires a radical break in development, which Laufer conceptualized as creating a subself (which he calls a self-system) to cope with the stress of war, and then trying to revert back to the former self after returning from the war. Laufer suggested that soldiers cope with this horrendous situation by constructing two "totally encapsulated self-systems that can function with reference to each other in antagonistic social matrices" (p. 38). In the terms of the present theory, the individual creates two subselves with minimal communication between them, a process similar to dissociation. The self is, therefore, discontinuous, and Laufer calls this state a serial self.

Although this process may result from any severe stressful situation, such as incest, rape or assault, warfare is especially stressful since Laufer points out that it is a process rather than an event. The trauma is repetitive and often continuous for long periods of time (weeks, months and years). The self must seek a structure that offers hope for survival while accepting death as a possibility and, for those in combat, Laufer labels this a "killer self." The content of this self clearly diverges from the self that existed in the past, back home. Soldiers may dehumanize the enemy, and some report eventually beginning to enjoy killing.

Returning home, soldiers may experience confusion and disorientation as they try to replace the war subself with the subself that they had before leaving for combat and which has had no chance to develop or mature during the war experience. One soldier reported to Laufer:

> I am trying to forget.....It's just like three years of a big void – a black spot in my life. I just cannot remember, or don't care to, what happened. It is like I was dead for three years there.

Laufer suggested, however, that the dissociation is not complete (as it is in the case of multiple personality). The two subselves do communicate with each other. Laufer saw the war subself as frozen in time, "a truncated self that survives in a timeless dimension of biographical time, able neither to evolve, integrate, not disintegrate" (p. 49). It is fixated on that time spent fighting, and its content is forever concerned with survival and death. Whenever the individual, back in America, experiences moments of vulnerability, the war subself attempts to take over the mind, thereby creating "intrapsychic discontinuities and dualities that are inherently conflicted" (p. 49).

The former subself, which Laufer called the adaptive self, endeavors to integrate the person's identity across time, but has great difficulty doing this for the war subself. The individuals who fought in wars, therefore, remain structurally unstable because of the existence of these two antagonistic subselves. One Vietnam veteran said that, "I was two of myself, one human and the other inhuman. I delighted in destruction, and yet was a healer."

Because of this conflict, these individuals prefer to spend time with those who also fought, who understand them and whom they understand, while others try to communicate through memoirs and fiction. This communication is necessary to master the trauma, but it is not always sufficient.

The Nazi Doctors

During the Second World War, the Germans set up concentration and extermination camps in order to eliminate Germans whom they judged to be unfit (such as the retarded and the mentally ill), Jews, Gypsies and other ethnic groups. Many physicians participated in these camps, helping in the selection of those who were to be exterminated immediately from those who could be sent to work, supervising the use of the gas, declaring the prisoners dead, and carrying out research projects on the prisoners.

Lifton (1986) argued that, in order to do this work, these physicians had to have a healing vision that they used to excuse their death-work. The healing vision was mostly involved with healing and purifying the Nordic race. The killing of those who were not Nordic or who were not good Nordic specimens was balanced by their experiments which gave them the ability to declare to themselves that they were scientists, even though the experiments typically killed the subjects of the research.

In order to explain the behavior of these physicians, Lifton proposed the concept of doubling, which he defined as the "formation of a part self, which ultimately becomes an entire and considerably autonomous self. Although the two selves are interacting parts of a holistic self, a dialectic exists between them......" (Lifton, 1988, pp. 28-29). It is this doubling that enables ordinary people to commit evil. Note, there is no amnesia between these two subselves, and so this is not multiple personality. Doubling is one way of adapting to a situation in which the individual is going to behave in an evil manner. For the German physicians, once they decided to work in the concentration and extermination camps, they had to use the process of doubling in order to adapt to the environment and to the work.

The prisoners at camps such as Auschwitz also used the process of doubling. One survivor told Lifton, "I was a different person in Auschwitz. I really was. I was a completely different person: (Lifton, 1988, p. 29), and some survivors had difficulty coming to terms with their "Auschwitz subself" once they had been rescued and returned to a non-Auschwitz life, much in the same way that the soldiers studied by Laufer above had difficulty re-adapting to civilian life.

THE CASE OF EDUARD WIRTHS

Lifton (1986) presented the case of Eduard Wirths who was appointed the chief physician at Auschwitz and who was a dedicated physician and described by inmates as conscientious, decent, polite and honest and yet also medicalized the selection process so that it was the physicians who met the trains of incoming prisoners and decided who would be killed immediately and who would be assigned for work. When Wirth surrendered in September 1945, the British officer shook his hand and commented to Wirths that now he had shaken the hand of the man who was responsible for four million deaths. Wirths hung himself a few days later.

Wirths was born in 1909 near Würzburg in southern Germany, the oldest of three boys. His father was a stonecutter. Under his father's influence, Wirths became meticulous, obedient and conscientious. He went into medicine and specialized in gynecology, but became a family physician. Nazi ideology appealed to him, and he joined the SA in 1933, and the SS the following year. He served in Norway in 1939 and on the Russian front until he was declared medically unfit in April 1942. He was sent to Auschwitz in September 1942 as the chief doctor because of his previous work for the state medical agencies and because the previous chief at Auschwitz had been unable to eliminate the typhus epidemics there.

As a good doctor, Wirths eliminated the epidemics in Auschwitz by disinfection procedures and by enlisting the inmates who were doctors to identify, isolate and treat inmates with typhus. He improved condition in the medical block and extended the work of the Polish and Jewish prisoner doctors. He protected his prisoner medical staff from abuse at the hands of the guards and stopped the practice of injecting prisoners with lethal phenol injections (by arguing that the prisoners fear of the injections and, therefore, the medical staff, hindered his efforts to prevent epidemics). He used his authority to claim several prisoners for his medical staff, and in 1944 he planned and supervised the construction of a new SS military hospital. Wirths, almost alone among the Auschwitz staff, kept to wartime food rations and often took stands against the brutality and random abuse of prisoners. Several inmates, after their liberation, had favorable memories of Wirths. This was Wirths' medical self at Auschwitz.

Soon after his arrival at Auschwitz, Wirths fought for medical control over the selections as the trains brought in prisoners. He won, and then he insisted in taking his turn doing selections rather than delegating them to subordinates. He could be "generous" – on one occasion, he was persuaded by his prisoner staff to "save" two thousand Jews from immediate death in the gas chambers, but a few days later, at a different subcamp, he selected two thousand others for the gas chambers. Wirths was a loyal and dedicated Nazi and was committed to the Nazi ideology concerning the superiority of the German race. This was Wirths' murderous Nazi self.

To counter his killing self, Wirths, also did research while at Auschwitz, as did other German doctors. He was interested in pre-cancerous growths of the cervix and he sent surgically removed cervixes to his brother's laboratory for further examination. Since the techniques used were new and the prisoners in poor medical health, there were usually complications and, if the inmates did not die during the procedures, they were sent to the gas chambers.

Lifton noted that this division into two selves was functional for surviving in Auschwitz for people like Wirths but, once outside the confines of Auschwitz, after Germany's defeat, Wirths could no longer live with the doubling. Some of the other doctors, like Joseph Mengele, hid and then fled Germany. Many, like Wirths, killed themselves.

POSTSCRIPT

Reviewers and commentators view their job as categorizing (and criticizing) theories, and in the process noting their limitations and omissions. I decided to make their job easier by doing some of the work for them here in a final chapter, and I have relied on a fine analysis by Trevor Butt (2004) for the framework for this chapter.

UNDERSTANDING VERSUS EXPLAINING

Butt draws a distinction between understanding people and explaining their behavior. Hebb (1949) noted that we do not have to explain why people *behave*. As long as we are alive, we are always doing something. What we have to explain is the choice of behavior – why we do this rather that. So, causal explanations do not have to explain what "kick-starts" our behavior (as Butt describes explanation).

Some theorists see the causes of behavior (the determinants of our choices) as being in the mind, some in our genes and physiology, and others in the social forces that impinge upon us. The truth is usually a boring compromise of all of the alternatives, but theories tend to take extreme positions since that is the way to become noticed. I acknowledge the role of physiology and of social forces in determining the choice of behavior, but I have never been interested in those factors. I have always been fascinated by intrapsychic factors – the structures and processes in our minds. Multiple self theory, then, is an intrapsychic theory. It proposes mental structures that help us understand our behavior.

Are there causal factors in the theory? In Chapter 9, I have discussed developmental aspects of the theory, and our experiences from birth on clearly have an impact on our lives and, therefore, the development and nature of our subselves. But, despite the fact that multiple self theory does have causal elements, the theory primarily enables us to *understand* our behavior. It provides a vocabulary to describe our inner experience, to explore the experience in greater depth, and to provide tactics for changing the experience.

MIND VERSUS BODY

Many theorists, such as R. D. Laing (as well as Trevor Butt) dislike the dualism of considering the mind as body as separate entities. They prefer to conceptualize individuals as mind-body amalgams. In that view, the mind and body "are not separate sets of events, but separate constructions of the same events.....We should talk about being bodies rather than having them" (Butt, 2004, pp. 37, 99).

I consider the choice between viewing the mind and body as separate entities or as a holistic combination a construction that people accept for themselves. I assume that theorists such as Laing and Butt "feel" that their minds and bodies are one. I had a friend who, when I asked her, "How are you doing today?" would give me her estimate of her blood sugar level. I assume that she felt one with her body. Fritz Perls in his Gestalt therapy liked to have his client "own" their bodies. Instead of saying, "My eyes keep looking away from you." He had clients say, "I keep looking away from you."

In contrast, I "feel" that my body is an object that I have to contend with. I often comment, as I get older, that, if my body were a car, I'd trade it in for new one. Sometimes I have the experience of being in a box of some kind (my body) and peering out at the external world through two holes cut into the side of the box (my eyes).

The resolution of mind-body dualism, then, is a personal, conceptual choice that each of us can make. But the two choices can be examined for the different predictions they make about human behavior to see which perspective leads to interesting predictions in different situations.

Butt argues that a dualisitic position inexorably leads to the problem of "ghost in the machine." "How does the ghost pull the levers of the machine?" (Butt, 2004, p. 36). I think not. Remember, since Donald Hebb's book in 1949, we do not have to explain how the ghost pulls the levers, but rather why the ghost pulls this lever rather than that lever.

Multiple self theory is not reductionist – it does not seek to find a neuropsychological basis for subselves. It accepts that multiple self theory is merely a set of concepts and processes that permit us to talk about our minds, but to do so in a way that does not force each us into a limited number of categories, but rather permits us to view ourselves and every other individual as a unique person, "similar to" but "different from" every other person.

THE INDIVIDUAL VERSUS SOCIETY

The two extreme positions here are that society is merely the result of separate individuals interacting versus that the behavior of individuals is merely the result of social forces acting upon them. In particular, *social constructivists* see the individual as being formed by societal structures. I often wonder whether social constructivists, who see the "self" as a social product and reject the humanistic notion of a self which gives us a sense of identity and uniqueness, apply their theory to themselves. Do they see themselves as having no stable identity, no central essence? If so, that seems rather sad. (I have a similar thought about Skinner who rejected internal mental states. Did he ever tell his wife or children that he loved them? Did he ever say that he was hungry?) It does seem to me that a theory of human behavior should be consistent with the theorist's own behavior, but some theories seem to "create" a monstrous individual.

Multiple self theory takes an individualistic position, but since mental structures are determined in large part by our experiences, it does not deny the important role of social forces.[25] Multiple self theory is *constructivist* in that it permits individuals to choose the way in which they conceptualize their mental states and, indeed, permits them to reject the theory (see Corollary 1a). But it is not *social constructivist*.

I would view these two extreme theoretical positions as reflecting the personal constructions of the theorists (and those who follow their theories). The social constructivists would seem to have a belief in an external locus of control (Rotter, 1966) while those taking an individualistic position have a belief in an internal locus of control.[26]

---

[25] Of course, the truth is that the individuals and the society have a mutual interaction in which they influence each other, and neither are the single, sole determinant of the other (Berger & Luckmann (1967).

[26] It is interesting that social constructivism is more popular in Europe than in America. In my years growing up in England and on my visits back, I have always been struck by how people there blame "them" for all the troubles – "them" being the government, big business or some other nation (America, Russia, the Middle East, etc.) – and this was often accompanied by a sense of helplessness. It was not my intent to emigrate (flee?) to a more individualistic society but, having done so, I am glad that I did.

We should note that even social constructivism does not eliminate the possibility of subselves. If the self is conceptualized "as a product of social interaction, we can see that very different selves might be produced at work, at leisure and with ones family" (Butt, 2004, p. 127). Even if people are different in different social contexts and "forged out of local social conditions" (Butt, 2004, p. 65), unless it is argued that a million different social contexts create a million different possibilities for an individual, then the social contexts, no matter how different they are, create only a few different possibilities for an individual. This is especially likely for social constructivists such as Gergen (1999) and Shotter (1993) who focus on the person in relation to others, for relationships can be categorized into a few (rather than an infinite number of) types. In social constructivism, it may be that, if "the self emerges through interaction and conversation" (Butt, 2004, p. 72), that there is no core self, but the constructivist approach of multiple self theory leaves the question of whether a core self exists up to the individual. Some individuals may have a core self, while others may not. As one of my friends once said to me, "David, superficially you appear to be deep, but deep down you're really shallow." He was implying, among other things, that I had no core self. I was merely a set of façade selves.

AND SO?

Regardless of how the multiple self theory of the mind may be categorized, the value of the theory is that it draws together themes that are present in many older theories of personality and extends those themes. It presents the theory in a series of clear postulates and corollaries that are explicit and can be examined theoretically, clinically and, possibly, empirically. Hopefully, the format here for the presentation the multiple self theory of the mind will open it to constructive alternatives (Kelly, 1955) that will result in a modified and improved theory.

REFERENCES

Allison, R., &Schwartz, T. (1980). *Minds in many pieces*. New York: Rawson-Wade.
Allport G. W. (1937). *Personality*. New York: Holt.
Allport, G. W. (1955). *Becoming*. New Haven, CT: Yale University Press.
Allport, G. W. (1961). *Pattern and growth in personality*. New York: Holt, Rinehart & Winston.
Altrocchi, J. (1999). Individual differences in pluralism in self-structure. In J. Rowan & M. Cooper (Eds.) *The plural self* (pp. 168-182). London, UK: Sage.
Anderson, R. E., & Carter, I. E. (1974). *Human behavior in the social environment*. Chicago: Aldine.
Anderson, R. I. (1985). Current trends in survival research. *Parapsychology Review*, 16(6), 12-15.
Angyal, A. (1941). *Foundations for a science of personality*. New York: Commonwealth Fund.
Angyal, A. (1965). *Neurosis and treatment*. New York: Wiley.
Arkin, R. M. (1981). Self-presentation styles. In J. T. Tedeschi (Ed.) *Impression management theory and social psychological research* (pp. 311-333). New York: Academic.
Assagoli, R. (1975). *Psychosynthesis*. London: Turnstone.
Baumeister, R. F. (1998). The self. In D. T. Gilbert, S. T. Fiske & G. Lindzey (Eds.) *The handbook of social psychology, Volume 1* (pp. 680-740). Boston: McGraw-Hill.
Beck, A. T. (1976). *Cognitive therapy and emotional disorders*. New York: International Universities Press.
Bénabou, R., & Pycia, M. (2002). Dynamic inconsistency and self-control. *Economics Letters*, 77, 419-424.

Berger, P., & Luckmann, T. (1967). *The social construction of reality*. Harmondsworth, UK: Penguin.
Berne, E. (1961). *Transactional analysis in psychotherapy*. New York: Grove, Press.
Berne, E. (1964). *Games people play*. New York: Grove Press.
Bernstein, M. (1956). *The search for Bridey Murphy*. New York: Pocket Books.
Bogart, V. (1994). Transcending the dichotomy of either "subpersonalities" or "an integrated unitary self." *Journal of Humanistic Psychology*, 34, 82-89.
Bonarius, J. C. J. (1970). Fixed role therapy. *British Journal of Medical Psychology*, 43, 213-219.
Boulding, K. E. (1968). *The organizational revolution*. Chicago: Quadrangle.
Bourguigon, E. (1976). *Possession*. San Francisco, CA: Chandler & Sharp.
Bowen, K. (1971). Principles and techniques of multiple family therapy. In J. Bradt & C. Moynihan (Eds.) *Systems therapy* (pp. 187-203). Washington, DC: Georgetown University Press.
Buckley, W. (1967). *Sociology and modern systems theory*. Englewood Cliffs, NJ: Prentice-Hall.
Bull, D. L. ((2001). A phenomenological model of therapeutic exorcism for dissociative identity disorder. *Journal of Psychology & Theology*, 29, 131-139.
Burnett, C. (1986). *One more time*. New York: Avon.
Butt, T. (2004). *Understanding people*. New York: Palgrave Macmillan.
Butt, T., Burr, V., & Bell, R. (1997). Fragmentation and the sense of self. *Constructivism in the Human Sciences*, 2(1), 12-29.
Campbell, J. D., Trapnell, P. D., Heine, S. J., Katz, I. M., Lavallee, L. F., & Lehman, D. R. (1996). Self-concept clarity . *Journal of Personality & Social Psychology*, 70, 141-156.
Casteneda, C. (1972). A separate reality: Further conversations with Don Juan. New York: Pocket Books.
Cattell, R. B. (1948). Concepts and methods in the measurement of group syntality. *Psychological Review*, 55, 48-63.
Cervone, D. (2005). Personality architecture. *Annual Review of Psychology*, 56, 423-452.
Chiari, G., & Nuzzo, M. L. (1996). Psychological constructivism. *Journal of Constructivist Psychology, 9, 163-184.*
Claus, P. J. (1979). Spirit possession and spirit mediumship from the perspective of Tulu oral traditions. *Culture, Medicine & Psychiatry*, 3(1), 29-52.
Cloninger, S. C. (2000). *Theories of personality*. Upper Saddle River, NJ: Prentice-Hall.

References

Corin, E. A. (1979). Possession psychotherapy in an urban setting. *Social Science & Medicine*, 13B, 327-338.

Csordas, C. J. (1987). Health and the body in African and African-American spirit possession. *Social Science & Medicine*, 24, 1-11.

Davidson, D. (1985). Deception and division. In J. Elster (Ed.), *The multiple self* (pp. 79-92). New York: Cambridge University Press.

De Sousa, R. (1976). Rational homunculi. In A.O. Rorty (Ed.), *The identities of persons*. Berkeley, CA: University of California Press.

Deaux, K. (1991). Social identities. In R. C. Curtis (Ed.), *The relational self* (pp. 77-93). New York: Guilford.

Dennett, D. C. (1978). *Brainstorms*. Brighton, England: Harvester.

Eliot, T. S. (1952). *The complete poems and plays 1909-1950*. New York: Harcourt, Brace & World.

Ellis, A. (1962). *Reason and emotion in psychotherapy*. Secaucus, NJ: Lyle Stuart.

Elster, J. (1985). *The multiple self*. New York: Cambridge University Press.

Epstein, S. (1979). The stability of behavior. *Journal of Personality & Social Psychology*, 37, 1097-1126.

Epstein, S. (1983). The stability of confusion. *Psychological Review*, 90, 179-184.

Erikson, E. H. (1968). *Identity: youth and crisis*. New York: Norton.

Erikson, E. H. (1959). Identity and the life cycle. *Psychological Issues*, Monograph No. 1. New York: International Universities Press.

Evans, R. I. (1981). *Dialogue with C. G. Jung*. New York: Praeger.

Ewing, K. P. (1990). The illusion of wholeness. *Ethos*, 18(34), 251-278.

Eysenck, H. J. (1967). *The biological basis of personality*. Springfield, IL: Charles Thomas.

Eysenck, S. B. G., Eysenck, H. J., & Barrett, P. (1985). A revised version of the psychoticism scale. *Personality & Individual Differences*, 6, 21-29.

Fairbairn, W. R. D. (1954). *An object-relations theory of the personality*. New York: Basic Books.

Federn, P. (1952). *Ego psychology and the psychoses*. New York: Basic Books.

Festinger, L. (1957). *A theory of cognitive dissonance*. Palo Alto: Stanford University Press.

Firestone, L. (2004). Separation theory and voice therapy methodology applied to the treatment of Katie. In D. Lester (Ed.) *Katie's diary: Unlocking the mystery of a suicide* (pp 161-186). New York: Brunner-Routledge.

Firestone, L. (2005). Voice therapy. In R. I. Yufit & D. Lester (Eds.) *Assessment, treatment, and prevention of suicidal behavior* (pp. 235-277). Hoboken, NJ: Wiley.

Firestone, R. W. (1988). *Voice therapy*. Santa Barbara, CA: Glendon Association.
Firth, R. (1969). Foreword. In J. Beattie & J. Middleton (Eds.) *Spirit mediumship and society in Africa* (pp. ix-xiv). New York: Africana.
Fitzpatrick, M. A. (1988). *Between husbands and wives*. Beverly Hills, CA: Sage.
Fitzpatrick, M. A., & Ritchie, L. D. (1994). Communication schemata within the family. *Human Communication Research*, 20, 275-301.
Flavell, J. H. (1963). *The developmental psychology of Jean Piaget*. New York: Van Nostrand.
Flournoy, T. (1900). *From India to the planet Mars*. New York: Harper.
Fransella, F. (1995). *George Kelly*. London: Sage.
Freud, S. (1933). New introductory lectures on psychoanalysis. New York: Norton.
Frick, W. B. (1993). Subpersonalities. *Journal of Humanistic Psychology*, 33, 122-128.
Gardner, M. (1957). Fads and fallacies in the name of science. New York: Dover.
Geertz, C. (1984). From the native's point of view. In R. A. Shweder & R. A. LeVine (Eds.), *Culture theory* (pp. 123-126). Cambridge, UK: Cambridge University Press.
Gergen, K. (1999). An invitation to social constructivism. London: Sage.
Gergen, K. J. (1971). *The concept of self*. New York: Holt.
Gladding, S. T. (2007). *Family therapy*. Upper Saddle River, NJ: Pearson.
Goff, D. C, Brotman, A. W., Kindlon, D., Waites, M., & Amico, E. (1991). The delusion of possession in chronically psychotic patients. *Journal of Nervous & Mental Disease*, 179, 567-571.
Goffman, E. (1961) *Encounters*. Indianapolis: Bobbs-Merrill.
Goldstein, K. (1963a). *The organism*. Boston: Beacon.
Goldstein, K. (1963b). *Human nature in the light of psychopathology*. New York: Schocken.
Goncharov, I. (1954). *Oblomov*. Baltimore: Penguin.
Goodman, L. (1968). *Linda Goodman's sun signs*. London, UK: Pan Pooks.
Goulding, R. C., & Goulding, M. M. (1978). *The power in the patient*. San Francisco: TA Press.
Goulding, R. C., & Goulding, M. M. (1979). *Changing lives through redecision therapy*. New York: Brunner/Mazel.
Haley, J. (1971). *Changing families*. New York: Grune & Stratton.
Hebb, D. O. (1949). *The organization of behavior*. New York: Wiley.
Heenan, D. (2002). *Double lives*. Palo Alto, CA: Davies-Black Publishing
Hermans, H. J. M. (2002). The dialogic self. In Y. Kashima, M. Foddy, & M. J. Platow (Eds.) *Self and identity* (pp. 71-99). Mahwah, NJ: Lawrence Erlbaum.

Higgins, E. Y., Klein, R., & Strauman, T. (1985). Self-concept discrepancy theory. *Social Cognition*, 3, 51-76.

Hofstadter, D. R. & Dennett, D. C. (Eds.). (1982). *The mind's I.* Brighton, England: Harvester.

Horowitz, M. (1988). Formulation of states of mind in psychotherapy. *American Journal of Psychotherapy*, 42, 514-520.

Iida, J. (1989). The current situation in regard to the delusion of possession in Japan. *Japanese Journal of Psychiatry & Neurology*, 43, 19-27.

Jackson, D., & Weakland, J. (1961). Conjoint family therapy. *Psychiatry*, 24, 30-45.

James, W. (1890). *Principles of psychology*. New York: Holt.

Janis, I. L. (1972). *Victims of groupthink*. Boston: Houghton-Mifflin.

Janov, A. (1972). *The primal scream*. New York: Dell.

Jaroff, L. (2001). Talking to the dead. *Time*, 157(9), 52.

Jones, C., & Shorter-Gooden, K. (2003). *Shifting*. New York: HarperCollins.

Jourard, S. M. (1971a). *The transparent self*. New York: Van Nostrand.

Jourard, S. M. (1971b). *Self-disclosure*. New York: Wiley.

Jung, C. G. (1977). *Psychology and the occult*. Princeton, NJ: Princeton University Press.

Kampmann, R., & Hirvenoja, D. (1978). Dynamic reaction of the secondary personality induced by hypnosis to the present personality. In F. H. Frankel & H. S. Zamansky (Eds.) *Hypnosis at its bicentennial* (pp. 183-188). New York: Plenum.

Kazdin, A. E., & Wilson, G. T. (1978). *Evaluation of behavior therapy*. Cambridge, MA: Balinger.

Kelly, G. A. (1955). *The psychology of personal constructs*. New York: Norton.

Kelly, G. A. (1965). The language of hypothesis. In B. Maher (Ed.) *Clinical psychology and personality* (pp. 147-162). New York: Wiley.

Kenny, M. G. (1981). Multiple personality and spirit possession. *Psychiatry*, 44, 337-358.

Kilmann, R., & Thomas, K. (1975). Interpersonal conflict handling behavior as reflections of Jungian personality dimensions. *Psychological Reports*, 37, 971-980.

Klimo, J. (1987). *Channeling*. Los Angeles: Tarcher.

Koestler, A. (1967). *The ghost in the machine*. London: Hutchinson.

Koslowski, S. W. J., & Ilgen, D. R. (2006). Enhancing the effectiveness of work groups and teams. *Psychological Science in the Public Interest*, 7, 77-123.

Krippner, S. (1987). Cross-cultural approaches to multiple personality. *Ethos*, 15, 273-295.

Laing, R. D. (1969). *The divided self.* New York: Pantheon.
Laing, R. D. (1982). *The voice of experience.* Harmondsworth, UK: Penguin.
Lang, J. M. (2007). Crafting a teaching persona. *The Chronicle of Higher Education.* February 9, C2.
Laufer, R. S. (1988). The serial self. In J. P. Wilson, Z. Harel, & B. Kahana (Eds.) *Human adaptation to extreme stress* (pp. 33-53). New York: Plenum.
Lester, D. (1985). Applications of the principles of group dynamics to systems theories of personality. *Psychology,* 22(2), 1-3.
Lester, D. (1992). The disunity of the self. *Personality & Individual Differences,* 13, 947-948.
Lester, D. (1995). *Theories of personality.* Washington, DC: Taylor & Francis.
Lester, D. (1997). Multiple selves and self-monitoring. *Perceptual & Motor Skills,* 84, 938.
Lester, D. (1998). Phenomenological description of subselves using George Kelly's Repertory Grid. *Perceptual & Motor Skills,* 86, 537-538.
Lester, D. (2003). The plural self. *Perceptual & Motor Skills,* 96, 370.
Lester, D. (2005). Is there life after death? An examination of the empirical evidence. Jefferson, NC: McFarland.
Lester, D. (2007). A subself theory of personality. *Current Psychology,* 26, 1-15.
Lewin, K. (1935). *A dynamic theory of personality.* New York: McGraw-Hill.
Lewin, K. (1936). *Topological psychology.* New York: McGraw-Hill.
Lewin, K., Lippitt, R., & White, R. (1939). Patterns of aggressive behavior in experimentally created "social climates." *Journal of Social Psychology,* 10, 271-299.
Lifton R. J. (1970). *History and human survival.* New York: Random House.
Lifton, R. J. (1986). *The Nazi doctors.* New York: Basic Books.
Lifton, R. J. (1988). Understanding the traumatized self. In J. P. Wilson, Z. Harel, & B. Kahana (Eds.) *Human adaptation to extreme stress* (pp. 7-31). New York: Plenum.
Loevinger, J. (1971). *Ego development.* San Francisco: Jossey-Bass.
Lubchansky, I., Egri, G., & Stokes, J. (1970). Puerto Rican spiritualists view mental illness. *American Journal of Psychiatry,* 127, 312-321.
Lycan, W. G. (1981). Form, function and feel. *Journal of Philosophy,* 78, 24-50.
Lynne, G. D. (2006). On the economics of subselves: Toward a metaeconomics. In M. Altman (Ed.) *Handbook of contemporary behavioral economics* (pp. 99-102). Armonk, NY: M. E. Sharpe.
Maddi, S. R. (1972). *Personality theories.* Homewood, IL: Dorsey Press.

References

Mair, J. M. M. (1977). The community of self. In D. Bannister (Ed.), *New perspectives in personal construct theory* (pp. 125-149). New York: Academic.

Margolis, H. (1982). *Selfishness, altruism and rationality*. New York: Cambridge University Press.

Markus, H., & Nurius, P. (1986). Possible selves. *American Psychologist*, 41, 954-969.

Markus, H., & Wurf, E. (1987). The dynamic self-concept. *Annual Review of Psychology*, 38, 299-337.

Marriott, J. (1984). Hypnotic regression and past lives therapy. *Australian Journal of Clinical Hypnotherapy & Hypnosis*, 5, 65-72.

Maslow, A. H. (1942). Self-esteem (dominance feeling) and sexuality in women. *Journal of Social Psychology*, 16, 259-294.

Maslow, A. H. (1970). *Motivation and personality*. New York: Harper & Row.

McAdams, D. P. (1985). The imago. In P. Shaver (Ed.), *Self, situations and social behavior* (pp. 115-141). Beverly Hills, CA: Sage.

McCulloch, W. W. (1965). *Embodiments of mind*. Cambridge, MA: MIT Press.

McNair, D. M., Lorr, M., & Droppleman, L. F. (1971). *Profile of Mood States*. San Diego: Educational & Industrial Testing Service.

McRae, R. R., & Costa, P. T. (1999). A five-factor theory of personality. In. L. A. Pervin & O. P. John (Eds.) *Handbook of personality* (pp. 139-153). New York: Guilford.

Meade, G. H. (1934). *Mind, self, and society*. Chicago: University of Chicago Press.

Mehrabian, A. (1968). *An analysis of personal theories*. Englewood Cliffs, NJ: Prentice-Hall.

Meichenbaum, D. (1977). *Cognitive-behavior modification*. New York: Plenum.

Meichenbaum, D. (1985). *Stress inoculation training*. New York: Pergamon.

Meichenbaum, D., & Cameron, R. (1974). The clinical potential of modifying what clients say to themselves. In M. J. Mahoney & C. E. Thoresen (Eds.) *Self-control* (pp. 263-290). Monterey, CA: Brooks-Cole.

Merton, R. K. (1968). *Social theory and social structure*. New York: Free Press.

Miller, J. G. (1965). Living systems. *Behavioral Science*, 10(July), 93-237.

Minsky, M. (1986). *The society of mind*. New York: Simon & Schuster.

Minuchin, S. (1974). *Families and family therapy*. Cambridge, MA: Harvard University Press.

Mischel, W. (1968). *Personality and assessment*. New York: Wiley.

Mischel, W. (1993). *Introduction to personality*. Fort Worth, TX: Harcourt Brace Jovanovich.

Mischel, W., & Peake, P. K. (1982). Beyond déjà vu in the search for cross-cultural consistency. *Psychological Review*, 89, 730-735.

Mischel, W., & Peake, P. K. (1983). Some facets of consistency. *Psychological Review*, 90, 394-402.

Moldoveanu, M., & Stevenson, H. (2001). The self as a problem. *Journal of Socio-Economics*, 30, 295-330.

Monte, C. F., & Sollud, R. N. (2003). *Beneath the mask*. Hoboken, NJ: Wiley.

Morris, W. (Ed.) (1976). The American heritage dictionary of the English language. Boston: Houghton Mifflin.

Morse, N. C., & Reimer, E. (1956). The experimental change of a major organizational variable. *Journal of Abnormal & Social Psychology*, 52, 120-129.

Murray, H. A. (1938). *Explorations in personality*. New York: Oxford University Press.

Murray, H. A. (1959). Preparations for the scaffold of a comprehensive system. In S. Koch (Ed.), *Psychology, Volume 3* (pp. 7-54). New York: McGraw-Hill.

Neruda., P. (1970). *Selected poems*. New York: Delacorte Press

Ogilvy, J. (1977). *Many dimensional man*. New York: Oxford University Press.

Ouspensky, P. D. (1949). *In search of the miraculous*. New York: Harcourt, Brace & World.

Parini, J. (2005). *The art of teaching*. New York: Oxford University Press.

Pasricha, S. K., Murthy, H. N., & Murthy, V. N. (1978). Examination of the claims of reincarnation in a psychotic condition. *Indian Journal of Clinical Psychology*, 5, 197-202.

Pattison, E. M., & Wintrob, R. M. (1981). Possession and exorcism in contemporary America. *Journal of Operational Psychiatry*, 12, 13-20.

Pears D. (1985). The goals and strategies of self-deception. In J. Elster (Ed.), *The multiple self* (pp. 59-77). New York: Cambridge University Press.

Perlmutter, D. D. (2008) Get another life. *The Chronicle of Higher Education*, March 14, C2-C3.

Perls, F. S. (1969). *Gestalt therapy verbatim*. Moab, UT: Real People Press.

Perls, F. S. (1976). Gestalt therapy verbatim: Introduction. In C. Hatcher & P. Himelstein (Eds.) *The handbook of gestalt therapy* (pp. 21-79). New York: Jason Aronson.

Perls, F. S., Hefferline, R. F., & Goodman, P. (1951). *Gestalt therapy*. New York: Julian.

Platman, S. R., Plutchik, R., Fieve, R. R., & Lawlor, W. G. (1969). Emotion profiles associated with mania and depression. *Archives of General Psychiatry*, 20, 210-214.

References

Polster, E. (1995). *A population of selves*. San Francisco: Jossey-Bass.
Progoff, I. (1973). *Jung's psychology and its social meaning*. Garden City, NY: Anchor.
Progoff, I. (1975). *At a journal workshop*. New York: Dialogue House.
Pullman, P. (1995). *The golden compass*. New York: Alfred A. Knopf.
Raskin, J. D. (2002). Constructivism in psychology. In J. D. Raskin & S. K. Bridges (Eds.) *Studies in meaning* (pp. 1-25). New York: Pace University Press.
Reid, A., & Deaux, K. (1996). Relationship between social and personal identities. *Journal of Personality & Social Psychology*, 71, 1084-1091.
Rich, A. (1981). *A wild patience has taken me this far*. New York: W. W. Norton.
Richards, D. G. (1990). Dissociation and transformation. *Journal of Humanistic Psychology*, 30(3), 54-83.
Richeport, M. M. (1992). The interface between multiple personality, spirit mediumship, and hypnosis. *American Journal of Clinical Hypnosis*, 34, 168-177.
Ring, K. (1992). *The Omega project*. New York: William Morrow.
Rogers, C. R. (1959). A theory of therapy, personality, and interpersonal relationships, as developed in the client-centered framework. In S. Koch (Ed.) *Psychology: A study of a science, Volume 3* (pp. 184-256). New York: McGraw-Hill.
Rogers, T. B. (1981). A model of self as an aspect of the human information processing system. In N. Cantor & J.F. Kihlstrom (Eds.), *Personality, cognition and social interaction* (pp. 193-214). Hillsdale, NJ: Erlbaum.
Rorty, A. O. (1985). Self-deception, akrasia and irrationality. In J. Elster (Ed.), *The multiple self* (pp. 115-131). New York: Cambridge University Press.
Rotter, J. (1966). Generalized expectancies for internal versus external control of reinforcement. *Psychological Monographs*, 80, #1.
Rowan, J. (1990). *Subpersonalities*. London, UK: Routledge.
Sampson, E. E. (1983). Deconstruing psychology's subject. *Journal of Mind & Behavior*, 4, 135-164.
Sandbek, T. J. (1993). *The deadly diet*. Oakland, CA: New Harbinger.
Satir, V. (1967). *Conjoint family therapy*. Palo Alto, CA: Science and Behavior books.
Schelling, T. C. (1978). *Micromotives and macrobehavior*. New York: Norton.
Schwartz, R. C. (1995). *Internal family systems therapy*. New York: Guilford.
Sexton, T. L. (1997). Constructivist thinking within the history of ideas. In T. L. Sexton & B. K. Griffin (Eds.) *Constructivist thinking in counseling practice, research, and training* (pp. 3-18). New York: Teachers College Press.

Shaffer, L. (1947). The problem of psychotherapy. *American Psychologist*, 2, 459-467.
Shapiro, S., & Elliott, J. (1976). *The selves within you*. Berkeley, CA: Explorations Institute.
Shaw, M. E. (1976). *Group dynamics*. New York: McGraw-Hill.
Sheldon, W. H. (1942). *The varieties of temperament*. New York: Harper.
Shostrom, E. (1965). *Three approaches to psychotherapy*. Orange, CA: Psychological Films.
Shotter, J. (1993). *Cultural politics of everyday life*. Buckingham, UK: Open University Press.
Showalter, E. (2003). *Teaching literature*. Oxford, UK: Blackwell.
Sidgwick, H. (1893). *The methods of ethics*. London: Macmillan.
Simon, H. A. (1977). *An empirically based microeconomics*. New York: Cambridge University Press.
Snyder, M. (1987). *Public appearance/private realities*. San Francisco: Freeman.
Southgate, J., & Randall, R. (1978). *The barefoot psychoanalyst*. London: Association of Karen Horney Psychoanalytic Counsellors.
Steedman, I., & Krause, U. (1985). Goethe's Faust, Arrow's possibility theorem and the individual decision-taker. In J. Elster (Ed.), *The multiple self* (pp. 197-231). New York: Cambridge University Press.
Steiner, C. (1974). *Scripts people live*. New York: Grove.
Stevenson, I. (1977). The explanatory value of the idea of reincarnation. *Journal of Nervous & Mental Disease*, 164, 305-326.
Stevenson, I. (1988). Deception and self-deception in cases of the reincarnation type. *Journal of the American Society for Psychical Research*, 82, 1-31.
Stevenson, I., & Story, F. (1970). A case of the reincarnation type in Ceylon. *Journal of Asian & African Studies*, 5, 241-255.
Thalter R. H., & Shifrin, H. M. (1981). An economic theory of self-control. *Journal of Political Economy*, 89, 392-406.
Thouless, R. H. (1984). Do we survive bodily death? *Proceedings of the Society for Psychical Research*, 57(213), 1-52.
Toman, W. (1960). *An introduction to the psychoanalytic theory of motivation*. New York: Pergamon.
Trafimow, D., Triandis, H. C., & Goto, S. G. (1991). Some tests of the distinction between private self and collective self. *Journal of Personality & Social Psychology*, 60, 649-655.
Turner, R. (1978). The role and the person. *American Journal of Sociology*, 84, 1-23.

References

Van Dusen, W (1973). The presence of spirits in madness. In J. Fadiman & D. Kewman (Eds.), *Exploring madness* (pp. 118-134). Monterey, CA: Brooks/Cole.

Vargiu, J. (1974). Subpersonalities. *Synthesis*, 1(1), WB9-WB47.

Varma, V. K., Bouri, M., & Wig, N. N. (1981). Multiple personality in India. *American Journal of Psychotherapy*, 35, 113-120.

Viney, L. L. (1981). Experimenting with experience. *Psychotherapy*, 18, 271-278.

Wagner, E. (1971). Structural analysis. *Journal of Personality Assessment*, 35, 422-435.

Ward, C. (1980). Spirit possession and mental health. *Human Relations*, 33, 149-163.

Watts, A. (1961) *Psychotherapy east and west*. New York: Random House.

Weiss, E. (1950). *Principles of psychodynamics*. New York: Grune & Stratton.

Werner, H. (1957). The concept of development from a comparative and organismic view. In D. B. Harris (Ed.) *The concept of development* (pp. 125-148). Minneapolis: University of Minnesota Press.

Winnicott, D. W. (1960). *The maturational process and the facilitating environment*. New York: International Universities Press.

Woolger, R. J. (1988). *Other lives, other selves*. New York: Bantam.

Yablonsky, L. (1976). *Psychodrama*. New York: Basic Books.

Yalom, I. (1995). The theory and practice of group psychotherapy. New York: Basic Books.

Yap, P. H. (1960). The possession syndrome. *Journal of Mental Science*, 106, 114-137.

INDEX

A

abdomen, 26
abortion, 53
absorption, 142
academic, 147
accommodation, 62, 135, 136
accuracy, 113
achievement, 94
acute, 45
adaptation, 166
addiction, 97
adjustment, 36, 69
adolescence, 51, 103, 116
adult, 8, 44, 51, 79, 86, 96, 103, 117, 138
African-American, 145, 146, 163
age, xvi, 5, 8, 10, 58, 86, 88, 109, 112, 129, 132, 136, 140, 146, 161, 164
agent, 5, 13, 17, 108, 109
aggregation, 30
aggressive behavior, 166
alienation, 42
altered state, 106
alternative, 7, 21, 38, 52, 67, 71, 116, 131, 137, 140, 157, 160
altruism, 167
amalgam, 9
ambiguity, 37, 68
ambivalence, 37, 68, 69
amnesia, 105, 108, 109, 111, 113, 117, 154
analysts, 86, 139
anger, 48, 130, 146
anglo-saxon, 146
animals, 7, 109
anorexia, 88
antagonism, 114
antagonistic, 7, 152, 153
antecedents, 26
antisocial personality disorder, 37, 49
antithesis, 41
anxiety, 37, 39, 45, 48, 77, 99, 117, 123, 146, 147, 150
application, 127
argument, 29, 31, 50
arousal, 39
articulation, 135
artificial intelligence, 16
asian, 170
assault, 152
assertiveness, 62
assessment, 167
atlas, 149
atoms, 66
attitudes, 10, 20, 26, 28, 33, 46, 47, 68, 75, 76, 103, 136

auditory hallucinations, xvi, 109, 115, 117, 118
authority, 17, 20, 57, 155
autonomy, 11, 28, 33, 34, 62, 66, 67, 140, 141, 152
avoidance, 18, 62
awareness, 1, 22, 28, 38, 44, 45, 46, 48, 75, 92, 105, 108, 123, 137, 138

B

babies, 38
banks, 151
barriers, 11
beating, 84
bed-wetting, 40
behavior modification, 167
behavior therapy, 165
behavioral manifestations, xi
beliefs, 12, 40, 69, 106, 110
bell, 121
benefits, 12, 151
betrayal, 66
bipolar, 124
birth, 10, 85, 157
black women, 145
blame, 159
blood, 158
body language, 99
boys, 79, 155
brain, 7, 152
brainstorming, 102
breakdown, 1, 45, 51
brutality, 155
buddhism, 149
buddhist, 98, 139
bulimia, 88
bureaucracy, 110
burns, 108

C

cable television, 111
cannabis, 109
cardinal trait, 6, 7
cast, 4, 50
casting, 126
catatonia, 43
catatonic, 45
catharsis, 41
cathexis, 70, 73
catholic, 23
causation, 10
cell, 43
censorship, 73
certificate, 85
cervix, 155
chaos, 43, 91
cheating, 31
childhood, 19, 39, 51, 94, 95, 96, 103, 113, 118
children, 13, 21, 29, 36, 37, 38, 79, 86, 109, 112, 128, 137, 139, 146, 150, 159
Christmas, 151
civil war, 91
civilian, 154
class period, 147
classes, 30, 139, 148
classical, 151, 152
classical economics, 151, 152
classification, 19, 32, 125
classroom, 29, 31, 147, 148
cleaning, 85
cleavage, 76
clients, 20, 55, 58, 83, 84, 85, 86, 89, 92, 96, 97, 98, 100, 101, 102, 103, 104, 127, 150, 158, 167
closure, 5, 147
clusters, 52
coalitions, xiv, xvi, 59, 92, 98, 99, 101, 102
coconut, 114
codes, 146

co-existence, xiv, xvii, 34, 118, 142
cognition, 169
cognitive development, 143
cognitive dissonance, 126, 163
cognitive function, 143
cognitive process, 123
cognitive therapists, 122
cognitive therapy, 69, 98, 101
coherence, 4, 96
cohesion, 56
collaboration, xvii, 62, 142
collective unconscious, 2, 19, 74, 113
colors, 87
communication, 8, 11, 12, 43, 50, 57, 62, 78, 96, 99, 118, 119, 152, 153
community, 16, 33, 83, 107, 119, 146, 167
compensation, 45
competence, 17, 96
competition, 62
complement, xiv, 47, 53
complexity, 1, 58, 129
complications, 156
components, 10, 11, 74, 129, 138, 139, 141
composition, 4, 104
compulsive behavior, 37
concentration, 74, 153, 154
conception, 22, 39, 60, 125, 126, 137, 151
conceptualization, xv, 19, 33, 50, 65, 72, 118, 151
concrete, 19, 47, 65, 106
condensation, 23
conditioned response, 4
conductor, xiv, 59, 93
confession, 41
confidence, ix
configuration, 12
conflict, xv, 6, 8, 10, 14, 20, 27, 32, 33, 47, 48, 55, 56, 57, 60, 61, 62, 78, 90, 91, 97, 106, 141, 151, 152, 153, 165
conflict avoidance, 62
conflict resolution, 10, 62, 106
conformity, 57, 58, 62, 91
confusion, 37, 68, 69, 102, 153, 163

congress, vi
consciousness, 14, 15, 26, 29, 106, 115, 121, 141
constraints, 132, 151
construction, 99, 100, 122, 124, 126, 130, 131, 155, 158
constructivist, 101, 104, 121, 123, 126, 131, 132, 159, 160
consulting, 137
contamination, 71, 72, 73, 77, 84, 85
continuity, 11, 23, 33, 67
convergence, 6
conversion disorder, 9, 37
convulsion, 117
coping, ii
correlation, 30
costs, 151
counseling, xvi, 83, 169
counterbalance, 102
couples, 62
covering, 88
creativity, 91
credit, 31
criminal justice system, 61
criminals, 127
crisis intervention, 90
critical thinking, 63
criticism, 41, 79, 87
cross-cultural, 168
crying, 80
cultural beliefs, 106
cultural values, 5
culture, 20, 33, 66, 101, 106
curiosity, 33, 66

D

danger, 63, 96
data processing, 138
dating, 112
death, x, 28, 32, 38, 68, 84, 107, 111, 112, 113, 116, 118, 140, 153, 154, 155, 166, 170

decisions, xv, 11, 20, 28, 33, 56, 57, 58, 59, 60, 61, 62, 63, 79, 92
defense, 3, 10, 23, 39, 40, 47, 69, 122, 126
defense mechanisms, 3, 10, 23, 40, 47, 69, 122
definition, ix, xi, 138
deformities, 70
delusion, 47, 71, 72, 76, 77, 164, 165
denial, 47, 100
depersonalization, 72
depressed, 27, 53, 63, 94, 97, 102, 117, 123, 124, 130, 143
depression, 19, 40, 72, 73, 85, 92, 97, 123, 168
deprivation, 38
destruction, 42, 153
developmental psychology, 164
dichotomy, 149, 162
diet, 89, 169
differentiation, 6, 8, 9, 12, 44, 76, 135, 143
diffusion, 11
disability, 94
disappointment, 146
disclosure, 41, 165
discounts, 149
disinfection, 155
disorder, 4, 73, 88, 97, 109
displacement, 23
disposition, 5
dissatisfaction, 36
dissociation, 47, 76, 93, 105, 117, 118, 152, 153
dissociative disorders, 109
dissociative identity disorder, 105, 162
distortions, 122
diversity, 131
division, 9, 15, 156, 163
divorce, 80
doctors, 155, 156, 166
dominance, 11, 46, 167
doors, 116
dream, 13
drinking, 73
drug abuse, 19
drug use, 40
dualism, 158
duration, 12
duties, xv, 78
dynamic theory, 166
dysthymia, 37

E

earth, 100
eating, 40, 88, 97
economic theory, 61, 170
economics, 166
education, 67, 166, 168
ego, xi, 1, 2, 3, 5, 8, 11, 13, 17, 18, 19, 25, 35, 42, 51, 60, 69, 70, 71, 72, 73, 74, 75, 76, 77, 80, 84, 85, 86, 90, 99, 117, 138, 139, 142, 152
elderly, x
emotional, 3, 13, 34, 48, 49, 58, 62, 74, 122, 130, 146, 161
emotional disorder, 161
emotional responses, 49
emotional state, 58, 130
emotions, xi, xiii, xv, 15, 17, 22, 33, 38, 39, 49, 65, 69, 74, 80, 92, 97, 105, 127, 130, 136, 141, 163
empathy, 69
employees, 94, 148
employers, 53
empowerment, 103
encapsulated, 152
energy, 4, 32, 33, 55, 56, 70, 90, 91
engagement, 101
environment, 6, 8, 9, 13, 33, 38, 44, 45, 46, 48, 93, 126, 135, 143, 146, 149, 154, 171
epidemics, 155
epilepsy, 107
equilibrium, 8, 11
eros, 28
esthetics, 108

estrangement, 72
ethics, 170
ethnic groups, 154
ethnicity, 52, 145
evening, 145
evil, 38, 110, 154
evolution, 18
exaggeration, 146
excuse, 92, 154
expertise, 103
external influences, 15
external locus of control, 159
extraction, 129
extraversion, 26, 27, 30, 53, 58
extroversion, 75
eyes, 158

F

face-to-face interaction, 50
facial expression, 15, 59
factor analysis, 129, 130
failure, 6
familial, 66
family, xv, 10, 15, 23, 28, 33, 42, 62, 63, 66, 83, 91, 92, 94, 98, 99, 104, 107, 112, 114, 116, 119, 128, 129, 130, 133, 142, 155, 160, 162, 164, 165, 167, 169
family conflict, 62
family functioning, 104
family members, 98, 99, 128, 129, 130, 133
family physician, 155
family system, 23, 98, 169
family therapy, 23, 83, 98, 119, 162, 165, 167, 169
fat, 151
fatigue, 9, 77
fear, 21, 37, 39, 42, 43, 69, 93, 96, 102, 138, 139, 155
feedback, xi, 20, 32, 100, 147
feelings, 2, 3, 17, 20, 36, 38, 39, 40, 72, 74, 80, 90, 93, 96, 99, 123, 146, 152

fees, 67
females, 2, 74
femininity, 47
feminist, 147
films, 21
first world, 148
fishing, 86
five-factor model, 2
fluid, 6, 8, 9, 18
focusing, 5, 7, 9, 26
food, 68, 155
fraud, 108, 110, 112, 114
free association, 73, 89
freedom, 17
friction, 102
friendship, 66
frustration, 38
fulfillment, 109
fusion, xvii, 6, 118, 142

G

games, 84, 85, 86, 136
gas, 154, 155, 156
gauge, 147
gender, 3, 74, 146
generalized anxiety disorder, 101
genes, 157
gestalt, 16, 27, 36, 44, 53, 69, 95, 96, 97, 158, 168
ghost, 106, 109
gifted, 52
girls, 107
glasses, 55
goal-directed, 87
goals, 5, 39, 56, 57, 67, 68, 99, 140, 149, 150, 168
god, 28, 33, 66, 108, 109
government, 16, 159
grades, 38
graduate students, x
grandparents, 139

grants, 17
grids, 129, 130
group membership, 52
group processes, 16
group therapy, 96, 98
grouping, 11, 28
groups, xiv, 17, 23, 30, 47, 56, 57, 59, 61, 63, 79, 106, 118, 148, 154, 165
groupthink, 165
growth, 5, 33, 76, 103, 118, 124, 161
guardian, 107
guidance, 79, 118
guidelines, 100, 149
guilt, 40, 43, 109
gypsies, 154

H

hallucinations, xvi, 71, 72, 77, 105, 109, 115, 116, 117, 118
handicapped, 124
handling, 165
hands, 152, 155
harm, 11, 20, 33, 56, 92, 107, 142, 143
harmony, 11, 20, 56, 92, 142, 143
healing, 154
health, 22, 41, 42, 76, 92, 126, 141, 156
heart, 84
heavy drinking, 73
hebrew, 112
hegemony, 25
helplessness, 90, 159
heredity, 17
hierarchy of needs, 34
high school, 147
high scores, 118
hispanic, 23
holistic, x, xi, 3, 4, 7, 9, 36, 39, 40, 46, 51, 68, 69, 118, 152, 154, 158
holistic approach, x, 3, 152
homeostasis, 6
homework, 101

hospital, 85, 109, 155
hospitalization, 88
host, 108
hostility, 37, 41, 48, 69
house, 166, 169, 171
human, 2, 7, 9, 10, 29, 30, 33, 44, 60, 65, 74, 87, 109, 118, 122, 124, 136, 145, 151, 153, 158, 159, 166, 169
human behavior, 2, 9, 10, 30, 33, 44, 74, 122, 124, 145, 151, 158, 159
human information processing, 122, 169
humanistic perspective, 140
humanistic psychology, 3
husband, 52, 67, 85, 86, 142
hypnosis, 73, 110, 113, 165, 169
hypothesis, 27, 30, 105, 118, 129, 165
hysterical neurosis, 37

I

identification, 23, 91, 100, 114, 121, 136
identity, 1, 5, 11, 19, 21, 42, 43, 46, 47, 52, 94, 105, 108, 109, 116, 126, 153, 159, 162, 164
ideology, 62, 155
idiosyncratic, 39, 47, 88, 94, 106, 117, 124, 132, 140
illusion, 22, 23, 63, 163
images, 42, 97, 106
imagination, 49
imitation, xvi, 136, 137
immediate gratification, 49
impulsive, 70, 123, 150
impulsivity, 27
in situ, 102, 132
incentive, 151
incest, 152
incidence, 109
independence, 80, 101
Indian, 168
indicators, 29
indigenous, 23

Index

indigenous peoples, 23
individual differences, 29
individuality, 49
industrial, 16
inertia, 6
Infants, 15
infinite, 160
inherited, 5, 9
inhuman, 153
injections, 155
injunction, 86
injury, vi
inmates, 154, 155, 156
inner tension, 9
inoculation, 150, 167
insecurity, 4, 42
insomnia, 77
inspiration, 41
instinct, 32
instruction, 150
insulation, 12
integrated unit, 162
integration, xvii, 4, 5, 6, 7, 10, 11, 18, 19, 20, 22, 67, 76, 135, 141, 142, 143
integrity, 33, 43, 66, 143
intellectualization, 47
intelligence, 4
intentions, 5
interaction, xv, 8, 10, 20, 50, 63, 85, 113, 159, 160, 169
interface, 169
interference, 104
internal consistency, 4
internal organization, 12
international trade, 16
interpersonal relationships, 69, 135, 169
intervention, 90
interview, 21, 26, 113
intimacy, 41
introversion, 26, 30, 53, 75
intrusions, 71, 77
intuition, 26, 33, 53, 75
investment, 49

irrationality, 169
isolation, 4, 10, 12, 149

J

japanese, 165
jews, 154, 155
jobs, 137
judgment, 21, 22
Jungian, 19, 27, 113, 165
juries, 61

K

killing, 68, 78, 153, 154, 155
Korean, 63
Korean War, 63

L

labeling, 95
labor, 16
labor relations, 16
language, 46, 99, 122, 125, 165, 168
language skills, 125
laughter, 4
law, 16, 67, 148
leadership, 57, 58, 79, 91, 93
learning, ix, 5, 14, 15, 17, 29, 30, 31, 37, 48, 94, 96, 150
learning process, 96, 150
leisure, 160
liberation, 155
libido, 32
licensing, 96
lien, 48
life cycle, 163
life experiences, 8, 9, 111
life instinct, 32
life style, 137, 138
lifetime, 31, 151
likelihood, 44

limbic system, 152
limitations, 157
linear, 9
locus, 159
logical reasoning, 60
long period, 9, 27, 28, 30, 111, 153
love, 9, 19, 32, 33, 34, 35, 37, 44, 50, 52, 55, 66, 90, 123, 137
lover, 33, 123
lung cancer, 126
lungs, 149
lying, 52

M

magazines, 101
magnetic, vi
mainstream, 61
maintenance, 56
males, 2, 66, 74
management, 161
mania, 72, 168
manic, 130
manipulation, 7, 49, 109
marital conflict, 91
marriage, 91, 107
married couples, 62
mars, 164
masculinity, 47
mask, 2, 15, 50, 74, 168
maternal, 44
mathematics, ix
meals, 87
meanings, 121
measurement, 7, 30, 131, 162
measures, 29, 30, 58, 91
mediation, 18, 97
mediators, 27, 99
medications, 107
medicine, 155
meditation, 98, 149
membership, xiv, 23, 52

memory, 3, 107, 111, 118
men, 58, 83, 107, 129, 152
mental health, 171
mental illness, 166
mental state, 159
mentor, ix
messages, 86, 110, 111, 116
metaphor, 16, 21, 23
microeconomics, 170
microscope, 65
middle ages, 113
Middle East, 159
military, 155
mind-body, 158
mirror, 148
misunderstanding, 147
models, 51, 52, 60, 148
mold, 103, 121, 147
molecules, 66
money, 137, 151
mood, 27, 30, 117
moral judgment, 46
morning, 145
morphogenesis, 11
motivation, 46, 170
motives, 5, 60
mouth, 26, 88
movement, 11, 53, 142
multiple personality, xvi, 11, 67, 105, 107, 108, 109, 111, 117, 118, 153, 154, 165, 169
multiplicity, 12, 13, 17, 23, 61, 92, 93, 94
murder, 68, 87
muscles, 40
Muslims, 108
myopic, 151

N

naming, 16, 89, 95, 96
narcissistic, 70
nation, 159
natural, ix, 21, 23, 91, 107

Index

natural sciences, ix
negative consequences, 102
nervousness, 67
network, xvi, 92, 98
neuroses, 48
neurotic, 36, 37, 38, 39, 40, 41, 42, 44, 45, 48, 49, 69, 76, 106
neuroticism, 27, 58
nightmares, 107
noise, 87, 121
non-human, 108
nonverbal, 77
normal, 7, 19, 44, 108, 110, 117, 130
norms, 63, 91
novelty, 108
nuclear, 6
nurturing parent, 90

O

obedience, 91
objectivity, 69
observations, 23
obsessive-compulsive, 37, 38
old-fashioned, 70
opposition, 2, 74
optimism, 41
oral, 43, 143, 162
oral tradition, 162
organ, 39, 68
organism, 5, 7, 45, 164
orgasm, 33, 107
orientation, 43, 58
ownership, 101

P

pain, 38, 86, 87, 94, 118
paranoia, 73
parents, 3, 13, 19, 29, 37, 38, 39, 42, 44, 45, 47, 85, 86, 91, 92, 103, 112, 116, 123, 128, 137, 139
passenger, 11
passive, 48, 95
pathology, 7, 22, 70, 72, 73
patients, 7, 39, 41, 47, 109, 115, 116, 127, 130, 135, 150, 164
peer, 57, 136
perception, ix, 3, 4, 12, 40, 44, 45, 46, 111, 113, 114, 122, 123, 125, 131, 138
perfectionism, 51, 97
permeability, 70, 73
permit, 11, 41, 48, 49, 75, 96, 159
perseverance, 46
personality dimensions, 165
personality disorder, 40
personality test, 127
personality traits, 18, 29, 31, 52, 95, 114
pessimism, 41
phallic stage, 143
phenol, 155
philosophers, 12
philosophical, 47
philosophy, 5, 6, 109
photographs, 137
physicians, 154
physics, ix, x, 125
physiological, ix, 6, 30, 34, 38, 66
physiological psychology, ix
physiology, 157
pig, 89
plagiarism, 113
planning, 49, 148
plants, 137
plastic, 66, 67
play, 2, 9, 15, 20, 23, 74, 83, 85, 86, 100, 118, 122, 123, 147, 162
pleasure, 19, 32, 33, 44, 94
pluralism, 22, 161
pluralistic, 62
poison, 85
polarity, 53
police, 50, 148
politics, 16, 170
poor, xi, 48, 49, 155

population, 169
positive regard, 44, 45
positive reinforcement, 90
positivism, 121
posture, 59
power, xiii, xiv, xv, 4, 5, 13, 14, 25, 26, 27, 28, 31, 32, 33, 51, 55, 57, 70, 77, 78, 81, 83, 90, 91, 95, 97, 99, 107, 108, 113, 116, 139, 141, 151, 164
preference, 10, 18
prefrontal cortex, 152
pregnant, 85
prejudice, 4, 72
pressure, xv, 16, 19, 56, 57, 62, 67, 68, 70, 77, 81
prevention, 163
primal fear, 39
prisoners, 154, 155
private, 52, 146, 170
proactive, 10
probability, 58
probe, 103
problem-solving, 47, 88, 91
pro-choice, 53
productivity, 57
professionalization, 47
Profile of Mood States, 130, 167
program, 32
pro-life, 53
propaganda, 16
property, vi, 128
proposition, 4, 15, 22
protection, 93
pseudo, 35, 36, 39, 40, 42, 69
psyche, 2, 74, 75, 76, 109
psychiatric disorder, 4, 109
psychiatric patients, 109, 115, 127
psychiatrist, 42, 84, 116
psychic energy, 70
psychoanalysis, 69, 90, 100, 141, 164
psychological health, xiii, 41, 68, 91, 119
psychological pain, 94

psychological processes, xi, xiii, 2, 7, 8, 17, 23, 25, 26, 45, 74, 124, 128, 138
psychological well-being, 22
psychologist, 16
psychology, ix, 7, 74, 121, 123, 163, 165, 166, 169
psychopath, 49
psychopathology, 43, 70, 78, 91, 164
psychopathy, 37, 73
psychoses, 49, 77, 163
psychosis, 36, 42, 43, 46, 76
psychosomatic, 40, 41, 79, 86
psychotherapeutic, xvi, 89, 90
psychotherapy, xvi, 13, 16, 19, 20, 26, 44, 55, 69, 74, 81, 83, 84, 89, 90, 93, 94, 95, 98, 100, 101, 102, 104, 106, 109, 123, 125, 127, 150, 162, 163, 165, 170, 171
psychotic, 41, 42, 44, 45, 76, 88, 106, 109, 113, 164, 168
psychotic symptoms, 41
psychoticism, 27, 163
public, 94, 102
Puerto Rican, 166

R

race, 154, 155
racism, 145
random, 155
randomness, 11
range, 11, 16, 19, 49, 58, 87, 124, 151, 170
rape, 152
ratings, 30, 130
rationality, 61, 167
reaction formation, 123
reactivity, 48
realist, 121
reality, 42, 46, 47, 63, 65, 108, 112, 122, 123, 126, 162
reasoning, 60, 88
rebel, 91
recall, 30, 112, 113, 130

reciprocity, 41
recognition, 20, 79, 92, 114
recovery, 113
reflection, 47, 88, 137
reflexes, 4, 5
regression, 6, 115, 167
regular, 101, 151
regulation, 149, 150
rehabilitation, 7
reincarnation, xvi, 105, 108, 111, 112, 113, 115, 118, 168, 170
reinforcement, 90, 169
rejection, 40, 41
relationship, xvi, 23, 42, 69, 88, 91, 92, 98, 103, 123, 131, 160, 169
relatives, 106, 114, 146
relaxation, 34
relevance, 84
reliability, 7
religion, 109, 110
religious groups, 106
religiousness, 114
repression, 36, 41, 47, 69
resistance, 1, 73, 78
resolution, 10, 62, 106, 152, 158
resources, 93
retirement, 140, 148
returns, 52
rewards, 30, 31
rigidity, 8, 9
role conflict, 23
rumination, 47
Russian, 155

S

sadness, 92, 130, 146
safety, 43
sample, 58, 109
sanctions, 11
satisfaction, xiv, 11, 28, 38, 58, 59, 62, 66
savings, 151

savings account, 151
scaffold, 168
schemas, 80, 103
schizophrenia, 42, 107
schizophrenic patients, 109, 135
scholarship, 147
school, 37, 67, 96, 124, 147, 148
scientific method, 121
scores, 58, 59, 118, 127, 129, 130
scripts, 19
search, 37, 44, 93, 112, 162, 168
Second World War, 148, 149, 153
security, 147
sedation, 109
segregation, 8, 52
self, i, iii, v, vii, 12, 15, 21, 22, 36, 49, 58, 100, 105, 121, 123, 127, 149, 151, 152, 161, 162, 164, 165, 167, 169
self-awareness, 22, 108
self-concept, 31, 45, 46, 49, 167
self-control, 108, 123, 151, 161, 167, 170
self-destructive behavior, 87
self-esteem, xv, 4, 80, 81, 97
self-help, 19, 101
self-identity, 5
self-image, 5
self-interest, 60, 61, 151
self-monitoring, 59, 166
self-observation, 150
self-organization, 90
self-presentation, 58
self-regard, 44, 45
self-regulation, 150
self-view, 80
seller, 112
sensation, 5, 26, 75, 93, 94, 97, 122
sensing, 26, 33, 53, 75
separate identities, 18
separation, x
series, x, 23, 88, 160
services, vi
severe stress, 152
sex, 31, 52, 109, 145

sex role, 31
sexism, 145
sexual activity, 34, 66
sexual behavior, 68
sexuality, 167
sexually abused, 88, 109
shade, 25
shame, 40, 99, 102, 146
shape, 31, 101
sharing, 62, 66, 67, 83, 141
shocks, 14, 123
short-term, 106, 151
signs, 55, 36, 164
similarity, 111, 151
skills, 5, 37, 49, 114, 125, 147
skin, 147
smoke, 41
smoking, 40, 126, 150
sociability, 27
social adjustment, 117
social attributes, 52, 53
social behavior, 167
social construct, 159, 160, 162, 164
social constructivism, 159, 160, 164
social context, 160
social control, 41, 123
social environment, 161
social group, xiv, 23, 33, 52
social hierarchy, 17
social psychology, 9, 161
social roles, 99
social situations, 131
social skills, 49
social structure, 167
socialization, 47
software, 13
soil, 42
sounds, 21, 87, 89, 92, 150
soy, 83
specialization, 12
speech, 87, 145, 146
speed, 11
spheres, 14

spiritual, 92, 146
spouse, 23, 32, 117
spreadsheets, 97, 101
SPSS, xi
stability, 31, 163
stages, 12, 19, 20, 90, 100, 143
standard deviation, 27, 59, 129
standards, 2, 3, 74, 91, 138
steady state, 6
stereotypes, 2, 74
stomach, 40
storage, 55
strain, 23
strategies, 69, 126, 150, 168
stream of consciousness, 50
streams, 5
strength, 29, 49, 65
stress, 76, 150, 152, 166
structuring, 102, 135
students, x, 9, 27, 29, 30, 58, 59, 68, 96, 128, 129, 146, 147, 148
subjective, 125
subjectivity, 123
sugar, 158
suicidal, 163
suicidal behavior, 163
suicide, 84, 88, 110, 163
suicide attempts, 84
superego, 3, 11, 13, 51, 117
superiority, 155
supervisors, 128
suppression, 100
surprise, 130
survival, 146, 153, 161, 166
surviving, 156
survivors, 154
switching, 117, 147
symbolic, 38, 39, 116
symptoms, xv, 4, 7, 26, 36, 39, 40, 41, 48, 67, 68, 70, 72, 76, 77, 78, 79, 81, 86, 107, 109, 113
syndrome, xi, 4, 106, 109, 111, 171
synthesis, 10, 19, 20, 76, 142

systems, xi, 2, 4, 5, 6, 8, 9, 10, 11, 12, 28, 39, 44, 66, 67, 68, 69, 74, 76, 84, 89, 90, 100, 104, 124, 125, 130, 131, 135, 139, 149, 152, 162, 166, 167

T

tactics, 69, 98, 104, 109, 150, 151, 158
taxes, 29, 31
taxonomy, 106
teachers, 136, 146, 147, 148
teaching, x, 146, 147, 148, 166, 168
teens, 107
television, 32, 33, 51, 111, 136
temperament, 170
temporal, 10, 12, 62
tension, 5, 8, 39, 40, 79, 91
tenure, 80, 146, 149
test scores, 30
textbooks, ix, x, 5
thanatos, 28
therapists, 21, 100
therapy, 16, 20, 38, 39, 44, 69, 86, 87, 88, 89, 90, 94, 95, 96, 97, 98, 99, 100, 107, 117, 150, 158, 161, 162, 163, 164, 167, 168, 169
thinking, 3, 15, 21, 26, 33, 34, 47, 52, 53, 58, 75, 76, 88, 122, 123, 125, 128, 136, 138, 169
threat, 43, 45, 116, 126, 137, 138
threatened, 43
threatening, 37, 38, 45
title, 27
tobacco, 149
torture, 43
trade, 16, 158
tradition, 107
training, 90, 150, 167, 169
traits, 1, 2, 4, 5, 6, 7, 52, 53, 95, 103
transactions, 84, 85
transfer, 90
transference, 23
transformation, 118, 169

transitions, 147
translation, 113
transparent, 165
trauma, 36, 93, 118, 138, 152, 153
trust, 20, 88, 93, 102, 143
tuberculosis, 109
twins, 55
typhus, 155
typology, 62

U

uncertainty, 37, 69
unconditional positive regard, 45, 89
undergraduate, ix, 27, 30, 58, 59, 128
unification, 5, 9
unions, 53
universe, 22, 66

V

validity, 7, 30
values, 5, 28, 45, 76, 79, 91, 136
variability, 30
variance, 29, 129, 130
varimax rotation, 129
vein, 7
vertical integration, 10, 66
video games, 136
village, 107, 114
violent, 116
vision, 154
vocabulary, 158
voice, 15, 33, 59, 76, 77, 79, 87, 88, 89, 99, 102, 110, 147, 150, 163, 166
vulnerability, 153

W

waking, 14
walking, 85
war, xv, 13, 76, 77, 78, 152, 153

warfare, 152
water, 28
weakness, 49
wear, 2, 50, 74
well-being, 22
wholesale, 3, 74
wind, 11
winning, 137
wives, 164
women, 58, 68, 125, 129, 145, 146, 167
working hours, 86
workplace, 145
world war, 148

worldview, 101, 104
writing, 40, 53, 58, 146, 147, 148

Y

young men, 152

Z

zen, 98, 139, 149